Google AdWords 2020

The Only PPC Advertising Guide You'll Need to Reach New Customers and Grow Your Business – SEO Beginners Guide Included

Eric Klein

Copyright © 2020 by Northern Press

All rights reserved. This book or any portion thereof may not be reproduced or used in any manner whatsoever without the expressed written permission of the publisher except for the use of brief quotation in a book review. The scanning, uploading, and distribution of this book via the Internet or via any other means without the permission of the publisher are illegal and punishable by law.

Please purchase only authorized editions of this book and don't participate in or encourage electronic piracy of copyrighted materials.

If you would like to share this book with another person, please purchase an additional copy for each one you share it with. This was hard work for the author, and he appreciates it.

Specific results mentioned in this book should be considered extraordinary, and there are no "typical" results. As individuals differ, the results will vary as well.

Published by Northern Press Inc.

Contents

Chapter 1: What Is Google AdWords and the Benefits of Using It...............6

Chapter 2: How to Set Up Your Own Google AdWords Account…..13

Chapter 3: Choosing Your Target Audience……..20

Chapter 4: How to Set Your AdWords Budget……..22

Chapter 5: The Steps to Writing Effective Ads…….26

Chapter 6: Picking the Right Keywords…..32

Chapter 7: Making Your Landing Page Effective for More Conversions……..39

Chapter 8: Your Google Quality Score: What it Means and How to Make It Higher……42

Chapter 9: How to Optimize Your AdWords Campaign…..45

Chapter 10: Running a Display Campaign……48

Chapter 11: Running a Shopping Campaign……52

Chapter 12: Creating a Video Campaign……57

Chapter 13: Creating a Universal App Campaign……63

Chapter 14: Linking Your Ad to Google Maps…..67

Chapter 15: Using the Keyword Planner…..72

Begginers SEO Guide…..79

Introduction

There are many different tools that you are able to utilize when it is time to work on your own advertising campaign. You need to create a product that is going to sell well with your target market. You need to find the right audience that you want to advertise to. You need to find ways that you can prove that you are better than the competition. Lastly, you need to pick out the right advertising channels to go with so that you can reach the most customers without spending a ton of money.

This guidebook is able to help you with many of these points—including how to pick out a good marketing channel to reach your customers. We will spend our time discussing the basics of Google AdWords—why it can make a big difference in the number of customers you are able to bring into your business as well as the number of sales that you get.

Google is one of the largest search engines in the world. Getting your ads on the first page of those search engines when customers are looking for you, or for products similar to what you sell, can be a top way of reaching your customers—and using Google AdWords for your campaigns is one of the best ways to do this.

This guidebook will take some time to talk about Google AdWords and the steps that you need to take in order to get the most out of your campaign. First, we will discuss what AdWords is and some of the benefits of using this marketing tool. We will then move on to setting up your own free AdWords account so that you are ready to take on the rest of the steps that are inside this book.

From there, we will take some time to look for the right target audience, and we will then have a discussion about how to set the budget for your campaign to get the most out of it. As you will see, you have to find a good balance of placing bids that will get your ad placed as high up on the page as possible—without spending more money than you need to in order to reach these goals.

Next, this guidebook will take a look at how to write ads that are effective and will *actually* entice your customers to pick you, how to do a good keyword search, and why effective landing pages do lead to conversions.

After you have written out the right types of ads and gotten your budget set and ready to go, there are a few other parts that a good marketer will need to use in order to *really* get your campaign off the ground and doing well.

In addition to the topics above, this book will spend some time talking about your Google Quality Score as well as how to make it higher to create more value out of your advertisement, how to optimize your AdWords campaign, and how to use the process of remarketing in order to get even more from each ad that you set up.

Are you an expert marketer who has been using other marketing tools for some time? We will even explore some of the tips that experts can use to make the most out of AdWords and all the campaigns that they do.

When you are looking for a new way to reach your customers and you want to be able to get the most out of each and every campaign that you start, then Google AdWords is the way to go. Make sure to check out this guidebook to help you get started with and get the most out of your Google AdWords campaign.

Chapter 1: What Is Google AdWords and the Benefits of Using It

AdWords is an online advertising platform that will send out ads—ones that are hyper-targeted—to potential customers who are looking for the services and the products that you offer. This tool is going to allow you a way to reach out to potential and future customers at the time it matters most, such as right when they are actively looking for you and your products.

There are many ways that you can advertise when you work with Google AdWords, but many businesses like to use the pay-per-click or PPC advertising. You can also pay per impression to your company as well.

When used on a mobile device, the ads are going to appear right at the beginning of the search result list. When you look at it on a laptop or other computer screens, these ads are going to be displayed on the top as well as on the right side of the result page of the search engine

AdWords will work to create ads that look similar to organic search engine results, but they will have a little box that is yellow and says "Ad" above or to the right of their page to differentiate them from the other searches on the page.

How Does AdWords Work?

There is a lot that comes with the AdWords system, but to keep it simple, we are going to make the setup process fit into three simple steps. These include:

1. Set the budget that you are comfortable with each day and the per click cap for the whole campaign.

2. Write out a brief ad that will let your customers know about what you are trying to offer.
3. Choose the right keywords that will ensure that Google is able to target the audience that you want for that specific ad.

Of course, there is more to it than that, but this helps to break it down. The other chapters in this guidebook will help to explore a bit more about this process and will provide you with the tools that you need to see some great results with your own Google AdWords campaign.

What Changes Have AdWords Seen Over the Years

Google started working with the AdWords system in 2000 as part of their monthly advertising services. The search engine originally ran campaigns for people who sent out information with their membership fees. However, Google was able to change the platform of AdWords over time in order to create a self-service setup where the users now have more control over the way that their marketing performs.

As AdWords has grown more in popularity, Google started to include some more features in the system. These features included things like listings for shopping, support for Google Maps, and more. In fact, AdWords has been integrated into almost everything that you can get from Google.

Google has also made changes in order to support advertising on mobile devices as well. In fact, Google has even gone through and increased the limits that people are able to use on their daily spend budgets. People can work with larger budget caps than before, which can be nice for those companies who are becoming more reliant on Google, and as the competition keeps increasing.

Every change that Google has done with AdWords throughout the years has been done with two intentions in mind. First, Google wanted to make it easier for people to control their campaigns. Second, Google is helping to make the content that is on AdWords show up in more places.

Recently, the number of searches that are done on Google has increased to more than 3.5 billion each day on average. This is compared to the 20 million searches that were done on the search engine in 2000. AdWords helps companies and individuals to get the most out of their searches and their marketing efforts easier to plan out.

Understanding How PPC Works

The pay per click, or PPC, setup, is part of the foundation that is found with Google AdWords. PPC is a popular form of online marketing where the advertiser is going to pay an amount of money each time that someone clicks on one of their ads. In other words, a website is going to pay in order to get the content listed on a search engine.

In order to do this, a business will need to create a brand new advertisement that will be able to show up on a search engine. This includes a unique description, a unique heading, and other extensions and data to make the ad easy to read through and enticing to the customer. The advertisement needs to be engineered in a way that it can draw attention, and hopefully clicks. Besides, the advertisement is able to appear on the top of a search provided that the keyword matches—and they place a high enough bid.

This is the opposite of using organic means to help the website become visible. Those who want to use PPC solutions must make sure that they are creating advertisements that are relevant and intriguing to their customers. We will explore a lot of the ways that a company is able to do that in the chapters that follow.

The amount that you will spend for every click on your website is going to vary based on what you want to spend, and the quality of the link. When you work with PPC, it is possible to receive a good return on investment, provided that the website is built in a way to encourage people to check it out. The most successful and attractive advertisements will be posted through AdWords for less money per click compared to ones that are just thrown together.

With PPC, you are able to spend as much or as little as you would like to ensure that your content stays visible online. You can even go in and create a limit on how much money you want to spend each day, week, or month with this kind of advertising. This ensures that your content will never go above your budget. When the monetary limit is reached, the ad goes offline.

You should consider working with PPC, especially when it comes to working with AdWords, in order to make your company noticed. Instead of spending a lot of time, even years, using traditional organic methods of making your site visible, you would then spend your money to get something that is instantly visible on Google. There are a ton of reasons why your business would want to try using PPC to get online and these include:

1. The competition for a keyword could be really high and intense. You might have to result in PPC tactics to become visible when you are marketing your work online.
2. You might have a website that is perfect and has all the organization that you need, but it may be true that you have nothing else to work with. Choosing your keywords within a new PPC campaign can be one of the best moves.
3. Maybe you should try to create a new advertising venture that will go beyond just using traditional post ads. Working with PPC is a great way to make sure that your content is intriguing.

4. Sometimes a business needs to be visible just to ensure that potential customers know what they do. Many ads with PPC are produced by newer or smaller companies who are trying to make it easier to spot their business as they try to grow.
5. A business might have a very specific type of promotion that they want to highlight with their customers. This could entail a limited time sale or even an introduction of a new product or a new service. A PPC is able to operate with the keywords that you choose to link with the new campaign.

PPC is a great field of work to undertake and each company is able to benefit from using it. When you decide to work with PPC on your next project, you may be surprised at how it can help your work become more visible than ever before.

What Are the Benefits of Using Google AdWords?

There are a lot of reasons why your business or company would choose to work with Google AdWords compared to some of the other options that are out there. Some of these benefits include:

1. Attract customers to your site right away: 90 percent of the searches done on Google are for products and services. When you use AdWords and get your page at the top of search results, you are making yourself more visible to your visitors so they are more likely to click on you and make a purchase.
2. Works faster than SEO: Providing your Ad Rank, which is a combination of ad copy, landing page quality, and bid for the ad, will be good enough to get your ads to appear right on the first page of the search results. SEO, on the other hand, can take months to implement and even then, your organic reach still may not make it to

the first page of search results. This helps you to reach your customers faster than ever before.
3. Find out what will convert for you: By linking together an Analytics account with your AdWords account, you are able to combine the reports from both in order to learn more about the marketing campaign and what seems to work the best for your company, and what you should avoid. For example, you can use these tools in order to eliminate certain keywords or ads that aren't really bringing you the conversions that you want during the campaign.
4. You can control the costs of advertising: When you work with AdWords, you will only need to pay for each time that someone clicks on the ad, not how often it shows up in a search result. This means that the business will only make a payment if there is actually a possibility that someone is interested because they clicked on the link. You get a chance to set your daily budget and can make sure that you don't go over budget just because someone glanced at the ad, without even clicking on it.
5. AdWords traffic is better with conversions than organic traffic: Recent studies have shown that clicks that occur through AdWords ads are more likely to lead to a conversion compared to those that come from the organic search results. This may be because these ads are directed to selling, rather than informing, and users are aware of this. Those who click on the ad copy may be more likely to purchase the product in the first place.
6. AdWords is taking over SERPS: You may think that no one clicks on ads. But when searchers are made with commercial keywords, 64.6 percent of the resulting clicks on ads. Do you really want to miss out on some of these potential customers because you think that no one clicks on advertisements?
7. Location targeting: Another benefit that you may enjoy is the idea of location targeting. Do you sell a product or

a service that is localized? With AdWords, you will be able to make sure that people in your location are the only ones who see your ads. For example, if you are a mobile computer repair business, it isn't likely that you want to reach people who are much out of your area to do your work. It is possible to just tell Google to only show these ads to those who are in a certain radius of your business, or even those who are just in your town. This keeps you in touch with the relevant customers and can make the campaign more effective.

AdWords is a great tool to use with your business. It helps you to reach your customers in a fast and effective way, one that works better than SEO and some of the other methods out there. You simply need to know about your target market, what keywords you would like to advertise with, and how much you would like to spend, and you are ready to go with your first campaign.

Chapter 2: How to Set Up Your Own Google AdWords Account

Before we get started with making some of our own campaigns, it is important to sign yourself and your business up with a Google AdWords account. The first step to do to make this happen is head to www.ads.google.com. When you create your account here, you have the option to use your own Google email account to help.

Since this is for your business and will be used in conjunction with your business, you should either come up with a unique email address to store all of the information that comes with this account or use your business email to do this. You don't want the information from AdWords to get mixed in with the personal emails you have.

Once your account has been established, there will be a few housekeeping items that you need to do. These won't take too long to do, you simply need to set in your time zone, the currency preferences, and some other settings to make sure that the account is ready to use.

Finally, you will end up on a page that will talk about your billing information. You have to fill this part out since you are responsible for paying Google for the advertising that they do for you.

With Google, there are two options that you can use when it comes to paying. The first option is the automatic payments. This one is going to make it easy to pay after you accrue some clicks. You will be charged once you reach a billing threshold (that you pick ahead of time), or 30 days after the last payment, whichever of those comes first.

Then there is the manual payment option. With this one, you will prepay Google Ads before the campaign even starts. Then these charges are taken out of that prepaid amount. Once the prepaid balance is gone, the advertising is going to be stopped for that campaign until you go in and make an additional payment.

With either option, you get the choice to have payments either drafted from a bank account or a credit card. Remember that Google needs to spend some time verifying your bank account, and this does take a few days to accomplish. If you want to get these campaigns off and going right away, then going with a credit card is the right option for you.

Setting Up the Campaign

This guidebook is going to go into more details when it comes to working with Google AdWords and how to create your own campaign. But this section is going to take a look at a few of the rules that you can follow when it comes to this, and how to get started on the right track.

The first thing that you can concentrate on is getting familiar with this new account. First, you may want to take a look at some of the terms that are common with a campaign so you make the right decisions. For example, an ad group and a campaign are seen as two different things in AdWords. An ad group is going to contain one or more ads that are going to share a targeted set of keywords. A campaign, on the other hand, will be a set of one or more ad groups that share a location targeting, budget, and other settings.

Spend some time going through the page and seeing if there are any terms that you don't know, and just getting a general familiarity when it comes to working on the site. You want to make sure that everything feels comfortable and makes sense before you get started.

The second step is to create the new campaign. We are going to take a look at an example of how to do this now. For this one, we are going to create a brand new campaign where we will target small business.

To get started with this, get into your AdWords account and then click on the blue + Campaign button. When you do this, you are going to see a list of all the different campaign types that you can choose. For this campaign, we are going o choose the ads to be at the top of Google Search Results so we will click on Search. You can take a look at the different options and decide what works the best for you.

From there, you will be asked to "Select the single goal that would make this campaign successful to you." There will be a few different options that you can pick from there, and you need to go with the one that makes the most sense for the campaign that you want to run and what your end goals are. For our example, we are going to choose leads because we are looking to use this campaign to get people to sign up for our free growth audits. And then we will answer that we would like to meet this goal with the help of website visits.

Next, we are looking to enter the name of the campaign in the field that says Campaign name. Now, you can also choose which network you would like to see these ads run on. You can decide whether or not you are interested in having the ad to be displayed on sites that are owned by the search partners of Google. This can help you to extend how far your ads reach.

While it is a good idea to use the display network of Google in some cases, we are going to stick with the Search Network for this ad. And to help save some money on this campaign, we are not going to let the ad be shown on the search partner sites.

During this process, you also need to select which languages and locations you want to target. You can make the decision on which area to target, such as a specific location, the United

States, or somewhere else. You have to customize this based on the needs of your company and what you would like the campaign to do.

Now, we are on to step three, where we are going to set the budget and the bid for our campaign. You have to come up with the bidding and budget strategy that seem to work the best for you. For this ad, we are working with a daily budget of $30 a day. This may seem low, but it is a place to start and you can always make adjustments to the budget based on how well it does. Don't click on the Accelerated Delivery method because you will want to have a little time in order to learn whether or not the ad is working.

The process of bidding on AdWords can be a bit complex for those who are not used to working on the system. There are several bid strategies that you can go with that are automated and that are meant to help you accomplish the right goals. If you click on the "Select a bid strategy directly" choice, you will then be able to choose to Maximize clicks, which will then set the bids to ensure you get as many clicks within your budget as possible.

Another option is to do a Target CPA (or cost per acquisition). This one is going to set up a bid automatically to help you get as many conversions as possible, while still making sure you reach your target CPA.

If you choose to go with the automatic bid strategy, Google is going to go through and set the bids for the campaign based on how likely the ad is to get a conversion or a click. The best part of using this kind of strategy is that Google will go through and do a lot of the work for you. However, since you are not the one who gets to directly control the budget amount, you may run through the money faster than usual.

The fourth step that you need to work on is to do scheduling. You can start out with this by selecting a start date, and then an end date. If you don't have an end date in mind, you can just select None for this and it will keep on running until you take it off. But if you want to promote a limited time offer or do a campaign that is seasonal, then make sure that you set an end date to make things easier.

As you go through this, you can see further down on the page that you can pick out the exact times and days that you want the ads to run on by creating your own schedule of your customers. You will only want to make it really customized if you have enough performance data out of a campaign to make sure the choices you make are completely optimized.

From here, we need to set up a campaign with Google AdWords for the first time. Try not to get overwhelmed by all the choices, and realize that you don't need all of them. For this campaign, we are just going to use a few of them. We are going to pay some extra attention to the Ad rotation option. This is important because if you are going to post more than one ad in that group, this allows you to have some more say in which ads are shown the most often.

We will talk about the next step in more detail later in this guidebook, but it is now time to select the target keywords you want to use. If you don't use the right keywords, all of the other work that we are doing with these campaigns is going to be a waste. Once you have done your keyword research, you will want to select a few keywords that will work the best with your ad group. But before we did this, make sure that you know the following match types:

- **Broad match**: This will allow the ad to show any time that someone searches for a phrase, similar phrases, plural or singular forms, stemming such as go and going, synonyms, misspellings, and other variations that are relevant.
- **Phrase match**: This is going to be the option that displays your ad in searches that exactly match the

phrase or ones that are close variations of that phrase that have additional words before or after, but never in the middle.
- **Exact match**: This one is going to only show your ad in searches that match the exact term or a very close variation.

You have to choose which of these you would like to use in order to see when your ads come out on search engines and when your potential customers will see the campaign that you are posting.

And now for this point, we are going to create the Ad. Remember that the ad group is where you are going to create at least one ad, but maybe more, and all of them will use a shared set of keywords. For this one, we are going to create three ads of text. To set these up, you must include an URL to your landing page or website. Then you can come up with three headlines, one for each ad. The headlines need to be no more than 30 characters, including those spaces, then separate each with the pipe character (|).

Once the headline is done, you can create a unique URL path. This is going to be a part of the display URL in the expanded text ads and it will often be seen right below the headline but above the description. This gives the potential customer a good idea where they are going to head to if they click on the ad.

And before you finish the ad, make sure that you write the two allowed descriptions to go with the ad. Each one can be 80 characters. This means you get a total of 160 characters in order to convince your customers to click on the ad and visit your website. This should talk about the business, talk about your product or services, and provide some value in another way.

Now that this is all set up, you can click Finish and create the ad, and it will be posted and start running based on the different parts that we have placed in this chapter. Remember that it could take a few hours before Google actually goes through and approves the ad and before you can start running the campaign. But as long as you have followed all of these steps and have filled in all of the information, there shouldn't be any issue with this and it won't be long before your ad goes live and starts to reach your potential customers.

Working with Google AdWords can be a great way to reach your customers in an effective way. These ads can reach your customers when they are most in need for you and when they are searching for products and services like what you offer. This makes them extremely effective and can help you get the conversions you are looking for.

Chapter 3: Choosing Your Target Audience

The next thing we are going to take a look at is how to choose your target audience. This can make a big difference in the type of campaign you are able to work with, where you should target the campaign, and even what products and features you should advertise.

Once you already know the product and services that you would like to work with, you then need to come on to figuring out the target market for the business. The target market is going to be the audience or customer group where you are trying to sell the product or service as well.

You will find that it is impossible in order to get every customer who fits into that target market, working to make your services and products are geared towards this group, and writing ads that match up with them can be so important. Let's take a look at some of the steps that you need to take in order to figure out your own target market before creating an AdWords campaign.

The first thing that you can do is analyze the different features that you are offering with your products and services. You can then determine the benefits that a customer will be able to get from that product, or how that particular product or service will fill the needs of your customers. You can sit down and write down these features to make the analysis a bit easier.

When you have the features all done, you can look at the customers and figure out which ones are the most likely to purchase the product, and also use the services that you provide. Consider a lot of different demographics when you are trying to come up with this target customer. Some demographics that you can consider include ethnic background, gender, educational level, occupation, marital status, income level, gender, and age. Identify which of these categories about the customer will have the biggest need for the product that you are selling.

Another thing that you can consider is the personal characteristics of the potential customers you want to work with and then determine how the lifestyle of the customer will affect their need to have your product. For example, you may want to figure out the personality traits, values, and interests of your customer to help you as well.

During this analysis, you also need to take a look at the competition and the market they are targeting as well. You can analyze the needs that the competition is already meeting for the customer. Then you can look through the market and see if there are any areas in the market that have been overlooked. If you can, this is where you need to market yourself and seek to fill the void within the market, rather than wasting your time and your money trying to target the market that your competition is already meeting.

If you already have a business that is in operation, it is time to look through the current customers that you have. You can take a look at the products and services that seem to interest your current customers the most, and then determine what benefits the customers get from these particular products. You can then take the time to market in the same manner to your potential customers.

Now that you are done bringing out all of your research, compile it together to look through a bit better. Use these findings in order to figure out who in the market has the most need for the products that you are selling. And try to keep the market in good balance so that you have a nice sized target market, one that isn't too big and also isn't too small at the same time.

Chapter 4: How to Set Your AdWords Budget

Now that we are ready to go, it is time to figure out how much you should budget for your AdWords campaign. The budget is one of the first decisions that you need to make when it comes to setting up the AdWords account. You want to make sure that you are able to pick out a budget that is effective—one that doesn't waste any money—but will still be enough to reach the customers that you want. Some of the points that you should consider when it comes to picking out the AdWords budget includes the following:

Fees

The first thing to see with your AdWords budget is that there isn't a flat or an annual fee. There also isn't any setup charge for having an AdWords account. Instead, you will need to set up the campaign, and then submit a bid for it. The overall goal here is that Google is going to show your ad when people search for your chosen keywords. This means that you need to place a bid that is high enough that your ad will be placed in the right spots and that will reach your customers.

When you work with AdWords, you won't pay anything until a customer actually clicks on the ad. Each time that the ad gets a click, Google will assess a per click fee against your account. This is why it is known as pay per click advertising. If no one clicks on your ad, you won't end up paying anything. If you get a lot of clicks, you have to pay for those clicks, but you will also earn sales from the products that you sell through the ad.

Bids

When you get to the setup screen of AdWords, you will get a chance to determine how much you want to bid for your clicks.

You also get the option of letting AdWords pick out the bid. If you pick out the latter option, Google will suggest a good bid price, and if your ads bring in traffic at that price, then that is good news for you. The good news is that you can always go back into the account later on and then change the bid to a new level later on if it isn't working for you.

Ranking

Next thing to consider is the ranking of your ad. The bid amount that you choose is going to give you a good idea of how the AdWords account will rank the ad. Google does this process in order to make money. So, the higher you can make your bid, the more likely it is that your ads will show up right at the top of the page.

Let's say that there are two companies who are bidding to make an ad with the same keywords. Both come up with ads that are engaging and compelling. But one of those companies will bid a higher amount for those keywords. Which one do you think is the most likely to end up right at the top of the page.

Remember when you work on bids, this is a bidding platform where you are going to bid against all the other competitors for the top spots. And just like when you do SEO that is organic, the position on AdWords is going to matter. The ads that end up in the top three spots are going to get a ton more clicks and sales compared to those that end up further down or end up on the right side of the page.

Budgeting

Another thing that you have to keep in mind when you do this is that it's possible that Google could run your daily spend up to 20 percent past the budget that you specified. This means that if you set out your budget each day to be at $30, then it is possible that Google will run your ad until you spent $36 for the day, especially if it ends up being a traffic-heavy day for the keyword. Google does this in order to make it easier to maximize any sales opportunities during periods of high traffic for your keywords.

However, there will be some balance when it comes to this variance when it comes to the monthly charging limit. If you have a daily budget that sticks with $30 a day, Google won't bill you above $912 (which is $30 multiplied by 30.4 days on average a month), when the month is up. Your monthly charging limit is an important number for you to pay attention to if you want to operate the account on a tighter budget.

In the long run, the bid amount and the amount you spend each day will be up to you. Your goals for the ad campaign needs to dictate the bid and the budget amounts. You can pick out a number that you are the most comfortable with. Start out with one amount and try it out for a bit. After some time, you can change the price to something else, or even suspend the campaign for a bit to give yourself some time to look over the strategy and make other decisions. As you see that the traffic increases and you work to make adjustments to the ads to ensure they are more effective, you will also see value in increasing the bid values and the daily budget.

If you have never worked with AdWords in the past, it is fine to start out with a more limited budget to give yourself some time to test out the waters. You can start out with a smaller budget so that you can test things out and see if there are any kinks that are in the advertisement. After you have some time to iron out all the kinks, you can release an ad with a higher budget to get the best results.

What Issues Will I Run into?

There is the possibility that a bottleneck is going to show up in your sales funnel and it is possible that this can happen any time between the prospect seeing the ad, deciding that they want to click on it, visiting the page, and then taking an action. It is important to be careful about this happening in order to avoid problems later on.

One area where you are going to need to be careful about is the wording of the ads that you post. Finding ways to write an ad that is effective, enticing, and succinct is hard to do and you may have to go through and rewrite the ad a few times before you are able to find the one that seems to work the best with your customers.

Creating the wrong bid price can be a problem as well. If you have the bid price too low, then you aren't going to get ranked high, and no one is going to spend the time looking at your ad. On the other hand, if you place a bid price that is too high, you will spend a lot of money on each click, and you may not get a good return on investment. Really research the bid price you should stick with, and experiment a bit in order to get the best results.

Figuring out a good budget when it comes to creating an ad campaign on AdWords can be difficult. You want to find the right mix between making a good profit and not wasting a lot of money in the process. But if you keep some of the tips in this chapter in mind, you will find that it is easier than ever to see some good results with your work.

Chapter 5: The Steps to Writing Effective Ads

Once you've had the time to go into your AdWords account and pick out the budget you would like to stick with, it is time to actually write out the ad copy for that campaign. These are the words that are going to *really* make your posting shine. They should include keywords and other words that will entice the customer to click on you rather than passing it by or choosing the competition.

Being able to write an ad that is effective will require a bit of creativity and a dash of science. There are right as well as wrong ways to go about this task. You don't have to be a professional writer to make these ads, but having some copywriting skills and knowing how to really sell your product can make a big difference.

The first thing that we need to look at are the four main components of successful ad copy. These four main parts will include:

The Headline

When you work in AdWords, you will need to stick below 30 characters. Try typing that out, including spaces. You will be surprised at how little space this is. Being able to come up with a brief and creative headline is critical, but it may take some practice and a few tryouts to see what you will use.

The main keyword that you are targeting should also show up in the headline because this is often the headline that the customer is going to search for when they want your product. The headline should also be a way where searchers can figure out that you are able to solve their problems.

Headlines are not the place where you will try to invoke curiosity or where you will try to be clever. For the headline to be successful, you want to speak right to the pain points of your customers and then establish that you are an authority in the field. You will find that your customers are more likely to take decisive action to help them avoid pain or discomfort than they will to accomplish any goal.

If you want to use some kind of pronoun in the headline, you need to keep it as some variation of You. You don't want to bring up the company or yourself either. Headlines that truly resonate with others, and help you to get a lot more clicks, are the ones that focus on the customer and not the company in the headline and in the other copy.

The Display URL

Once you have a catchy and useful headline, it is time to work on the display URL. This URL is going to appear right under the headline, but before any of the other copy that you are going add to the campaign. The URL that you place in this spot is the website that you want to increase the amount of traffic for.

Ideally, you will try to use a landing page for any product that you are looking to sell when you place the ad. We will discuss landing pages a bit later, but the landing page needs to be up and running, and in the best shape possible, in order to drive traffic to it. You don't want to waste your time paying to get people over to your site if they are going to be disappointed by what is there, or they aren't able to actually purchase something, and then they click away immediately.

The Description Lines

There are going to be two description lines and they are limited to just 80 characters each. You will only get a total of 160 characters to share the information that you want about a product, which isn't a lot of space overall.

In the first line that you get, make sure that you promote the service or the product that you want to sell, making sure that the main keyword is inside. Then, on the second line, remember that this doesn't always show up, especially with mobile devices. This is why the most important information should show up in the first line. Include special offers and other promotional information into the first line.

Be specific with the brief information that you are going to add to either of the description lines. Numbers can be a great way if you want to demonstrate how effective the service or product is. The same rule about pronouns is important in the descriptions as it was in the headlines.

A piece of advice that you can follow from ad guru John Kuraoka is "The second best word is 'you'. The best word is the customer's name". Since you aren't able to go out and get the name of every customer on the market who comes and looks at your ad, so using the term 'you' can be the best option.

The Final URL

The final URL is the other piece that you need to work on your campaign. The final one should match with the display URL. This is the page where the customer will be sent to any time they click on the ad. Make sure that you double check this and ensure that it is the actual page that you want the visitor to go to when they click on the ad.

Use the Power Words

Now that we know the four main components that come with a successful AdWords campaign, let's look at some of the other things that we need to consider when we are setting it all up. Since your AdWords ad is pretty limited on space, only 190 characters for the descriptions and the headlines including the spaces, that doesn't leave a lot of room for you to play with.

This means that you need to be careful with the words that you choose to go with.

The first thing to consider here is that you should choose words that are able to illustrate how the product is going to help solve the problem for the customer. Don't use this text space to ask questions that the customer can answer on their own. Focus on how the product you are selling will resolve their issues.

Let's look at an example of this. For a headline, you wouldn't want to list something that says "Got Gophers?" Of course, the customer has gophers. That is why they are searching for a product that will help them to remove the gophers that are in their yards. A better headline that serves the needs of your customers better and can make it more valuable to the customer might be "Remove Gophers Once and for All." This headline is going to tell your readers that if they click on the link, they are going to find a solution to resolve these gopher problems. This is what the customer is looking for in the first place, so make sure to provide it to them.

Another thing to try out is works like exclusive and limited. These help to generate some excitement and can persuade people to click on your ad right away, rather than waiting around. Many times people don't want to miss out on something that they see is amazing. This is known as fear of mission out or loss aversion. Using terms that are more time sensitive can be a great way to get people to click on the ad and make a purchase right away.

Those are just a few of the terms that you can use. You may also want to work with secret or free as a power word to get people to take advantage of the unique opportunity that you are offering to them. Most people don't want to miss out on a rare treasure or a deal.

A/B Testing

One more topic that we can discuss in this chapter, but can work with some of the other parts of your ad if needed, is known as A/B testing. When you are ready to prepare a new campaign with AdWords, you should do your best to come up with two ads that are strong.

If you write out two ads, both of which you think will be effective, and then you set them with the same keywords and the same budget, you can then run both of them for a few weeks, or another limited time, to see how each one is going to do for you.

The point of A/B testing is to check and see which ad is going to work the best for you. You can check out different headlines, different copy in the descriptions, and more. This is a good choice if you have two options, or even more, and you want to see which one is the strongest and most effective when it comes to doing the advertising.

Once both of them have been on the market for some time, you can see which one is the most effective. Then you will remove one of them and ramp up the budget that you want to use for the most successful one. The winner of that race is going to be the control ad. This is the one to beat. If you come up with more ideas,

Now, you can keep playing with the ads and see what works. If you have the resources and the second ad only lost by a little bit, for example, you can tweak it a bit and see if it will become successful as well. And if you have enough resources, you can do both of them until you get them right and see that it is the most effective.

When you are running one of these A/B tests, you should only change one element at a time. If you go through and change everything, or you change a bunch of things at once, it is hard to know what element actually made the improvements, or which one made things worse. When you only go through and change up one piece of the ad at a time, it is easier to tell how each of the individual changes performed in the ad for you and whether you should keep them or not.

After all, what is better than having one ad that is successful and going to bring in a lot of traffic for you? Two successful ads that can compete against each other and can constantly improve in order to bring in lots of traffic. If you use A/B testing in the proper manner, you will find that it is one of the best ways to get a good return on investment, and ensures that you will have the right copy to reach your customers each and every time.

The point of doing A/B testing allows you to focus all of your energy and your funds for advertising on the ad campaign that is going to provide you with the best return on investment. It may take a little bit of extra work, but it ensures that you really put out the ad that will bring in the biggest payoff and the best profits for you.

Chapter 6: Picking the Right Keywords

The next thing that we need to take a look at is how you can pick out the right keywords for your campaign. Before you do this campaign, you need to complete a thorough keyword research process. You can then use this research as you work on fine-tuning your landing pages and nearly any other online marketing materials you use. Consistent keyword use will be very important as you work through AdWords in order to get the best results.

It is very important for you to go through in order to do the legwork and get a list of keywords assembled before you set up the campaign at all. You will find that this is going to take up the most time when you are establishing an AdWords presence for your company, but it is so worth it. You will find that this work is going to help you see a better return on investment for the bids that you do on AdWords. Let's take some time to look at some of the steps that you need to do in order to do your keyword research to get the best results.

How Do I Start with My Keyword Research?

The easiest way for you to do this is to sit down and brainstorm a list of search terms that someone may use anytime they are looking for your product or company online. Start out with some basic and targeted keywords, and then you can work on your way out from there. These are going to be known as head terms.

These head terms are going to be brief, specific, but generic terms that people may use in order to find their way over to your website. For example, let's say that you just moved into a new home that has just dirt in the front yard. You may want to find someone in your area who is able to install new landscaping at the home. To do this, you may go on Google and search for things like landscaping company. This is a great head term that may be used by any company that installs and or maintains flowers, shrubs, trees, and grass.

You may find that picking out keywords that are one or two words long will cost more than going with a longer phrase. Longer phrases are going to be known as long tail keywords. These are more cost-effective when you are working on your campaign, and they can lead to a buyer who is more eager to purchase from you. Long tail keywords are just going to be head terms that embellished a bit, and they have become more and more important over time to the algorithms that are found in search engines. There are several ways that you can take a head term and turn it into a long tail keyword, and some of those methods include:

- Add in a geographical location. So you may pick out a keyword that says landscaping company in Nashville.
- Add in a specialty area. So you may pick out a keyword that says ornamental landscaping company.
- Add in other characteristics that can help identify your company. You may pick out a keyword that says family-owned landscaping company.
- Add in some comparisons to others. This may include a keyword like best landscaping company in Nashville.
- Add in some conditions that may be important to you and to the customer. This may include a keyword like affordable Nashville landscaper.

From here, you may find that you need to get even more specific about the services that you are looking for. Perhaps you are looking for something like artificial turf installers in Nashville. Or you could pick out a keyword like full-service landscaping in Nashville. Or Nashville landscaper that does tree removal.

With the long tail keywords, you may get a lower volume of website traffic than the head terms. But the ones who are searching in this manner and who click on you are going to be a better prospect for you. These customers are looking exactly for what you are offering, so you are more likely to get a sale from them.

Now, let's move back to the keyword research that you were looking at. Focus on the phrases that you think your customers would like to see any time they are looking for your service, product, or company, or anything that is similar. What sets you apart from the competition in the market, and what will drive customers to specifically seek what you are offering? Make sure that all of these are added to the long tail keywords on your list. The list may get longer in the beginning, but you can always cut it down a bit later.

What If I Can't Think of Good Keywords for a Business?

Then you need to search longer. There are hundreds or more search terms that you may use based on your circumstances. But when you spend too much time on your own product, sometimes it is hard to recognize the qualities that seem to set your company and product apart from the competitors.

One place that you should consider looking for input is from the past and the current customers and what led them to purchase and do business with you. This is something that you should already be doing for your business. All of that feedback can be important to some of your future marketing efforts and product improvements, but you need to have the information ahead of time.

Using Google Keyword Planner

There are many different online tools that you are able to work with in order to flesh out a list of keywords. Google's Keyword

Planner is a great option to choose because it is a free tool that is inside your AdWords account panel and is an easy resource. Simply enter in the list of keywords that you have, no matter how short it is, and then add them to the tool. The planner will be able to go through and generate out a list of additional keyword suggestions that you can work on as well.

Another aspect that you are going to enjoy when you work on the Keyword Planner is that it provides you with a ton of valuable data about each keyword. For example, you can get monthly search volumes, such as information on how many people searched for that keyword in the last month, the keyword difficulty, such as how hard it will be to use that keyword to reach the top of the first page of a SERPs, and more.

You are going to get dozens and even hundreds of keywords and even phrases that come up when you use this tool. Don't feel overwhelmed. Just look through a few of them and then pick out some terms that are the most relevant to your services, products, and company. It is not necessary to go through and use them all.

What About Using Branded Keywords?

If you are using products and services have branded names, then you need to do a bid on those keywords as well. Bidding on a branded keyword can be different than using a trademark in an actual ad copy, which is something that can get you into some trouble.

Even if you are the only company in the world that is selling something like "Super Deluxe Widgets" your competitors have a chance to bid on that keyword and can use their own ads in order to drive traffic over to theirs, and away from your own website. This may seem like a dirty and rotten trick, but it is allowed and completely legal. There isn't much you can do to stop them, except go after these keywords and use them yourself.

While there are some PPC experts that debate the benefits on going through and putting a bid on y our own brand name, most experts in AdWords say that you should include the company name, and the specific names of your products, in your keyword list.

One thing to note is that if you are doing your research and you find that a different company is using your trademark in their ad copy, then you can go onto Google and file a complaint to get that taken care of.

What Are Hummingbird-Friendly Keywords?

Hummingbird is an update that Google did to their algorithm. It was designed as a way to respond to the increased number of individuals who use their mobile and voice search technology rather than computers. When someone uses the voice search function on their phones, they are more likely to ask a full question, rather than do a keyword search. Hence, instead of typing in "super deluxe widgets," they would ask a question like "Where can I buy super deluxe widgets?" Or they may ask for something like "Who is the best full-service landscaper in Nashville? These full phrases are going to be known as hummingbird-friendly keywords.

To capture a lot of the mobile shoppers (which is a growing and growing part of your customer base), you need to make sure that these keyword phrases are a part of your campaign. Since mobile shoppers are not almost half of the online shopping share, you can't ignore these keywords so make sure that you have one or two, at a minimum, in place.

To help you add these keyword phrases to your list, think about the different ways that someone could ask their smartphone to find your website for them. Some of the angles that you can think about your company to make this work includes:

- Are your customers more likely to search for the company if they are near it?
- What is it about the product that people are the most drawn to?
- What is the most unique thing about your product?
- Are people more likely to search for the name of the product or your company?

Negative Keywords

AdWords also helps you to build out a list of negative keywords. These are the terms that you don't want the site to appear for when someone starts searching for you. This can narrow the audience down a bit by preventing your ad from showing up on the wrong search terms.

So, if you are a company that is selling Super Deluxe Widgets, you will want to make sure that your ad doesn't rank for Basic Widgets. There is no point going after the wrong customers and wasting time and money.

Paring Down the Keyword List

For the ad setup process, you need to choose somewhere between 10 to 20 keywords for the form. This doesn't mean that you should just come up with a ton of loosely related terms that have nothing to do with your site. If you have 20 really strong and good terms, then it is fine to use that many. But don't try to just fill them up because they are there.

When you are choosing the keyword group that you want to work within AdWords, make sure that they are closely related. The closer, the better with this one. Remember that your first ad has one really specific purpose and that is to drive traffic to one of your landing pages. You are selling just one product with this ad, so make sure that you choose keywords that are tied directly to that product.

Not only is this going to narrow down some of the keywords so that you can really hyper-target your ad to the right people, but it can help out with the Google Quality Score, something that we will discuss in more detail later on.

Even if you don't use all of the same keywords to work on your advertisement, make sure to keep that list on hand. You may not be able to use some of the terms right now, but you already did a lot of the work, and you may find those terms easier to use later on.

Chapter 7: Making Your Landing Page Effective for More Conversions

It is important to spend some time looking at the idea of a landing page in relation to how it works with the success of your AdWords campaign. When someone clicks on your ad, you will need to send them over to a landing page. This is basically the last place they are going to hit before they decide whether or not to take the next step and become your customer. This means that you need to take some serious time and really make a good landing page.

What Is the Landing Page?

A landing page is going to be some kind of page on your website where people will go to make purchasing decisions; in some cases, it can also be where they go in order to get the information needed so you can make buying decisions later. Your customer will be directed there from another website, an internal link on another page of your website, a social media link, or from one of your ads.

Landing pages should be where you are going to put the sales pitch for your product. These pages are where you will demonstrate exactly how you are going to solve the problem for your customer and try to convince them to click on the Buy button. Some of the things that you should ask yourself when considering what to add to the landing page includes:

- What do your landing pages need to look like in order to maintain the attention of your visitor?
- What do these pages need to tell customers in order to get the sale?
- What buttons, resources, and forms should be on the landing page in order to build up an email list, generate

the connections that you want on social media, or make an upsell?
- How do these landing pages convey a good and positive message for your company?

How Do You Optimize the Landing Page?

Before you go through and launch your AdWords campaign, you need to ensure that the landing page is optimized for the new amount of traffic that is going to flow in. When your ads usher in some new prospects to the website, the landing page that has been optimized will then convert more of those people into paying customers. Some of the things that should be included on an optimized landing page include:

- Easy to navigate: All of the drop-down menus need to be arranged and named in a logical manner. Contact forms and buttons should also be near the top of the page.
- Easy to scan and skim: Use lots of bullet points, lists, and sub-headers in order to draw in the attention of your reader to the major concepts on the page.
- Attractive: Try to use colors that are complementary and add in some images. You don't want to add in too much clutter though. Put in enough to attract the customer, but not enough to distract them from the main message.
- A call to action that is obvious: There should never be any room for guesswork when it comes to what you want readers to do on the landing page.
- Quick to offer a solution to the problem of the customer: To sell your product as a solution, you must use this page to paint a clear picture of the problem for your customer. Explain this to the customer and then show exactly how the product is going to be the solution they need.

- Well written: It is worth your time to have an editor look through the landing page to check for syntax, spelling, punctuation, and grammar errors. These may not seem like a big deal to you, but they could wipe out your credibility with customers.
- Consistent with the ads: The keywords that you added to the campaign should also show up on the landing page. Also, make sure that the same vibe, feel, and look are found on the landing page and the ads.

If you are trying to do everything on a tight budget, it may seem like a bad idea to hire outside help. But in reality, hiring a professional web designer to create or at least look through your self-made website can help. This ensures that you are able to improve the page as much as possible in order to get the sale.

The quality of your landing page and the relevance of the keywords that you pick are going to play a huge role when it comes to calculating out your Google Quality Score. Take the time that is needed in order to set up the website in a way that ensures it will generate sales.

To do this, make sure that the landing page is going to be attractive, logically laid out, and that it has all of the pertinent information that your customers will need to make the decision to purchase from you.

Chapter 8: Your Google Quality Score: What it Means and How to Make It Higher

One thing to remember about Google is that it is all about the numbers and the rankings. Every aspect of your campaign is going to be measured and assigned a place within the different algorithms that Google has. Nothing can be taken for granted when you are setting up your ad on Google because Google is always monitoring and calculating the performance of your data and because you need to be careful that changing algorithms won't mess with your ads.

No one wants to end up spending more on heir advertisement than they have to. And the Google Quality Score will help you to keep the costs of your campaign as low as possible. If you make ads that don't match up well, or do keyword stuffing or do other things that will anger your customers and make for a bad advertisement using AdWords, then your score is going to be lower and you will have to pay more for the keywords that you want to use.

However, if you make sure that you write high-quality ads for your campaigns, you follow the rules, you pick out good keywords, and you follow the other rules that come with Google AdWords, you will find that you will get a higher score. And this results in better bid prices, which gets you the visibility that you want, without the high costs.

Let's take a look at what the Google Quality Score is all about and how a marketer will be able to use this number to help effectively grow their audience without spending a ton of extra money.

What Is the Google Quality Score?

Each ad that is done on AdWords is going to be given a Google Quality Score. The keywords that go with your ad will be given this sore as well. Google has an algorithm that they use to determine if an add is doing well or not and some of the different aspects that will help you to get a higher score would include:

1. The CTR or click through rate, which is going to the be the percentage of people who click on the ad when they see it.
2. The relevance of the keywords to the ad. This is going to be a measure of how well the keyword will match with the text that you have in the ad.
3. The quality of the landing page. This is going to be determined by an evaluation of how the page is written and optimized, as well as the keyword and the ad relevance.
4. The quality and relevance of ad text to the keywords and the landing page.
5. The average account performance with AdWords over a given period of time.

So, why should you work on this quality score? A higher score can help to lower the amount you pay in bid rates, and it can ensure that the ad is going to rank higher. This means that you can get more out of your budget and get more customers to your page.

Ways That You Can Improve the Google Quality Score

The good news is that there are steps that you can take in order to improve the Google Quality Score that you have. And many of the topics that we have discussed so far in this guidebook will help you to get that score as high as possible. Some of the measures that you are able to take in order to maximize your ad performance and get the highest Google Quality Score possible includes:

- Keyword relevance: Make sure that the display URL and the ad copy are relevant to the keywords that you targeted.
- The relevance of the landing page: You should work to optimize your landing pages in order to give your visitors with a message and experience that's consistent with your ad.
- Test the different variations of the ad text to see which type of verbiage seems to get the best click-through rate.
- Build out the negative keyword list. This helps to narrow the target audience and ensures that you don't waste your budget on the wrong people.

To ensure that you get your ads placed in the best spots, and for a chance to get better visibility for less spending, you need to make sure that you have a boost to your Google Quality Score. The good news is that if you follow the tips in this chapter, and in the rest of the guidebook, you will naturally have a great Quality Score to help you out.

Chapter 9: How to Optimize Your AdWords Campaign

Now, when you take a look at AdWords, you will find that there are a number of bells and whistles that can be used in order to optimize the return that you get on your investment when advertising. Being able to utilize these tools to fine-tune the campaign and ensure that you are actually dialing into your specific target audience is something that will take a bit of time for you—but sticking with it and being a bit picky with some of the things that you choose with your ads can go a long way in helping you get the most out of your campaign. Let's take a look at some of the steps that you can take to help optimize your AdWords campaign.

AdWords Extensions

There are a variety of extensions that you can use in order to customize the information that shows up in your ads. These extensions are going to change the layout as well as the look of your ads depending on which one you choose. You have to figure out what data is the most important to some of your potential customers. Then you can use one or more of these options in order to get as much traffic as you can out of the campaign that you work with.

There are several extensions that you can work with. These extensions will include:

1. Callout extensions: These are nice because they allow you the chance to highlight the unique selling points about your product. These are going to be brief phrases that will appear below the description lines in your ad. They won't be linked, but they allow you to show some of the important aspects of the company right inside the ad.

2. Location extensions: These extensions will allow you to target your ads to a certain radius around their business location. Alternatively, you can choose a specific geographic area where you would like the ad to be shown. In addition, if you have a physical address, this extension will make it easier for the customer to know exactly where they need to go if they want to shop in person.
3. Sitelink extension: This one will create space underneath the primary ad for links to other pages that may be housed on that same website. If you think that sending the customer over to other pages on the same website would serve a good purpose as well, then this is something you should consider. For example, if you are working with shoppers who you know are not yet at the bottom of your sales funnel, then you know they want to do more research. Giving these customers some links to click on your website can help them to do a bit of research through the rest of the website.
4. Call Extensions: These extensions make it easier for a shopper to call your business directly. You will use this to place a call button right inside the ads. The call extensions are common when you are advertising to a mobile device. When you use this kind of extension, you are going to pay Google any time that someone clicks on this Call button.

Google is always changing things up and trying to enhance their extensions in order to fit the needs of both buyers and sellers. The best way for you to know what extensions are available and to keep up with everything is to get onto the AdWords account and look through the setup pages for ads. You never know when a new bell or whistle may show up there.

Keep Making Adjustments to Your Chosen Ads

Explaining all of the reports that are available with Google AdWords is something that could really fill up quite a few more books overall. While we won't go through and actually list out all of these right now, this basically means that there is a ton of information that is right at your fingertips when you get started with AdWords.

Being able to learn about and decipher all of this data can help you make the best decisions to bring in more profits. You can learn how to adjust your list of keywords, update the copy in your ad, fine-tune your budgeting to get the most out of your money.

There is only a little that you can prepare for when it comes to working with an online ad. In the end, it comes down to you as the advertiser being able to find the right combination of works, both in the ads and on your landing pages, that will lead to more people clicking and purchasing through the ads that you decide to place.

Think of all this as more of a work in progress. You are not going to be able to place one ad and then walk away and do nothing while you make a big profit. Even more advanced advertisers find that they need to make adjustments and change things until they reach the right mixture of what seems to work the best for your ad and your business.

Whenever you work on an advertisement, you will find that it is so important to figure out ways to optimize your content as much as possible. This makes it more likely that people are going to click on your ads, and can make it easier to actually make some sales on the clicks that you are getting.

Chapter 10: Running a Display Campaign

Now that we know some of the basics, we are going to get into more details about how to work with some of the different campaigns that you will want to run with Google AdWords. The first campaign type that we are going to pay attention to is a display campaign.

The Display Network that Google offers is going to be very convenient and worth your time, but to ensure that it works for you, you need to find ways to develop your own display campaign. This kind of display campaign will let you run a lot of ads online in various forms.

When you decide to work with this kind of campaign, you will offer pictures and other images that will link over to your site. You can also work with images that help you display the products that you are trying to sell or even things that will help illustrate the services you have to offer. Whatever you decide to use in your display campaign, plan out something that has a special and dynamic look to it so it has a chance to stand out from other advertisements.

How Do You Develop Your Display Campaign?

1. Click on the Campaign section of your AdWords account.
2. When you are there, click on the Plus sign in order to indicate that you want to set up a brand new campaign.
3. Select the display option.
4. List information on the goals of the campaign that you want to reach. You can choose to set one of the following as your goal:
    a. Drive in the sales. This is the best option when you have a basic product to sell.

b. Get some leads. This will happen through email sign-ups or other ways where you will collect contact information. Use this option if you have some services are high value and you want to market them.
c. Bring in website traffic.
d. Product or brand exposure. This helps to encourage people to take a look at your brand and see what it has to offer.
e. Brand awareness.
5. Choose a subtype to run the campaign with. You can choose to either go with a standard campaign or a Google campaign.
    a. The standard campaign is going to focus on having the ads appear on various sites that are in your Display Network.
    b. The Gmail campaign includes ads that can be shown to people as they look through their Gmail accounts. After you make your choice, you can't make changes to this section.
6. Enter your business website at this time. Google can provide you with some ideas for the keywords that you can use based on the site list that you have. You can then enter the keyword ideas will appear when you get your ad groups set up.
7. Enter in the name of your campaign.
8. Select the location that you wish to target. As you make adjustments to the location and to some of the other features, the approximate number of impressions that you get will either increase or decrease.
9. Enter the languages that you would like to use. AdWords can give you some recommendations based on the places you try to target. If you would like to target the United States and Canada, you may get a recommendation to add in French with the English.
10. Decide on the bidding campaign—a bit on the conversions, the clicks, or the viewable impressions.

11. List out the daily amount that you want to spend on your budget. Then set the delivery method for either accelerated or standard marketing. If this is your first campaign, then you should go with standard marketing. This gives you some time to work on the campaign and make sure that everything works the way that you want before you commit more.
12. Enter the name of the first ad group.
13. Include some information about the audience that you are most interested in reaching. You can choose to target the audiences based on how they interact with the content you have. You can focus the content on those who have already interacted with your content. You then have full control over what you do with the content in this case.
14. List out the demographics of those you would like to reach, such as gender, age, parental status, marital status, and household income. Which how the impressions to the campaign change based on these demographics.
15. Choose the placement that you want to use with the campaign. It is possible for you to go through and include specific websites. Enter the topic or the keyword that you would like to promote and then you can receive some recommendations that you can use for placements of the campaign.
16. Select the automation that you want to use with the campaign. The two choices are aggressive and conservative.
17. Add in the maximum cost you will pay for each click. There are also some other parameters that you can choose to use so look at those.
18. Now you can create a new ad now or you can click the Create Campaign button in order to get that ad applied in later on.

Creative an Ad That Is Responsive

When you decide to do an ad for this campaign type, you want to make sure that you are working on an ad that is responsive. This is a type of message that will concentrate on an image that adds a striking look that first with your message perfectly. To do this, you can go to the ad group where you would like to produce the ad, click on the option to add the responsive ad. And then put the image into it.

You have the option of uploading an image that you would like to use or to go through and scan your website for an image. You may also want to use the stock image that Google provides when you enter the URL. Be sure that whatever you plan on using is clear, effective, and you have the legal authority in order to use it.

As you go through the display campaign process, you will notice that there are a lot of different things that you can change along the way. You can change up the way that the advertising is displayed, the images that are there, the target audience and more. Take some time to mess around with these numbers a bit to help you see what is possible, and to ensure that you actually get the most out of your ad campaign.

Chapter 11: Running a Shopping Campaign

Another type of campaign that you can choose to work with is a shopping campaign. Have you ever looked through a listing where there were a lot of pictures that showed the products for sale? Maybe you were looking for a digital media player, and you saw a ton of pictures that went along the top. These pictures may have shown some of the most popular media players that are available on the market. Then, after you see the pictures, you will get information on the cost of the product, who sells that product, and the URL that you can head to in order to get to that player.

Marketing on the Google search engine is popular because it allows companies to share information on their products and services in a dynamic fashion. In addition, you can create your own shopping campaign to help make the content you sell more visible. Some of the steps that you can do in order to get a good shopping campaign started includes:

1. First, list a series of products that you are selling through AdWords.
2. Upload the images of your products, and include information like names, prices, and other things that the customer may want to know.
3. Place a bid on the keyword. Make sure that any keywords you use are relevant to the types of products you are selling.
4. People are going to see that your product is for sale when they find a keyword that relates to it. Remember that your product is going to compete with other products in the same field. For instance, if you are selling a pair of high heels through your shoe store, it is going to be displayed along with some of your competitors.

5. When someone clicks on the product or the picture, that customer is going to be sent over to your own site.
6. You will be charged for any click that comes into your site. You will earn a profit if the person who clicks ends up purchasing the item.

This shopping campaign is going to work well when you have physical products for sale. The benefit of using this kind of campaign is that it ensures that you get more qualified leads from the searches for your keyword. When you get in touch with people, they are going to notice that your products are of higher quality, and they can look at the pictures of your products to see all of the features before purchasing.

CPC Only

A shopping campaign is going to be considered a CPC only campaign. There are two ways that you will end up needing to pay when someone lands on your page and these methods will include:

1. The user will need to click on the ad that you post and then go to the landing page of the website that you specify.
2. Or the user can click on something that goes to a landing page for your local inventory. This a page that Google will host and provide to you.

The process for bidding on the keywords that you will use on this kind of campaign is the same with any other campaign that you use. The good news is that you will also have full control over deciding what you are going to spend on each click that a customer does to the website. You just need to make sure that you pay more than the advertiser behind you to ensure you end up on the first page of searches.

Where Will These Shopping Ads Show Up?

Your ads, when you use this kind of campaign, will appear on the typical search, as well as on some of the search partner sites. In either case, these ads are going to still be near the top of the search.

It is also possible for you to get your ads to show up on a Google Shopping search, assuming that it shows up in the right country. Google Shopping is a system where people are able to search for items and then get some detailed results on those products. If you want to be able to take a look at what Google Shopping is all about and why it can be a nice option, visit shopping.google.com

When you search for things on the Google Shopping page, you are going to find a ton of paid advertisements along the way. These ads will need to include all the details that the business has on a Google Merchant account, including details on the price, the business who sells it, the name of the product, and an image of that product.

Which Countries Can I Do This Campaign in?

Shopping ads and campaigns are not going to be available in all countries. Google will offer shopping campaigns in many major companies including the United States, Canada, United Kingdom, Australia, Japan, Brazil, Germany, France, South Africa, New Zealand, and Italy to name a few.

However, there are some major companies where this shopping campaign is not going to be available and you will have to find other marketing tools. Some countries where this service isn't available include China, Mexico, South Korea, Kenya, Egypt, Ivory Coast, and Luxembourg.

What Is Required to Run This Campaign?

Now, there are a few requirements that are needed in order to run this kind of campaign for your product. Some of the requirements for this kind of marketing option will include the following:

You need to have links to the Google Merchant Center and to AdWords.

The Google Merchant Center is important because it ensures that your content is available on Google. This is going to simplify the process because it allows you to upload all the data about your products for sale to Google. The setup will then let you send out information on photos, names, features, and prices to name a few. Basically, it makes it easier for your product to be found on a Google search.

To find out more about how all of this works, you need to go and visit merchants.google.com. You also need to take the time to link up the Merchant Center account with your AdWords account.

Your content needs to comply with Google shopping policies.

The policies are going to be similar to the rules that relate to content when you create links in your advertisements. You would be restricted as to what you can sell based on your physical location and who you are targeting. You also need to make sure that you aren't misrepresenting anything on your site, or you risk being removed and having your ad ineligible to work on this site.

You need to send in updates on a regular basis for the data on products.

You will need to update the information about your products once every 30 days in order to make sure that your listings will stay current. If you forget to do this, or you send incomplete information, then there is a risk of Google getting rid of the ads that you place.

The updates that you provide for the data on the products will also need to include some details on what types of products you are selling and how you plan to offer them to the public. Be sure that you add as much detailed information as you can on your products so that your campaign still shows up on the Google platform.

The product data specifications are going to be what you will use in order to get the content sent over to Google.

Depending on where you live, such as the European Economic Area, you need to be a member of CSS or Shopping Comparison Service.

Many CSS options are going to make it easier for you to manage your content, but in other cases, the CSS will have to run the campaign for you. Check with whichever CSS you are looking to work with and see what the rules are with that.

Working with a shopping campaign is a great way to list your products and showcase them in ways that really entice the customers that you want to work with. If you are selling a physical product and you want to be able to stand out from the competition, then this is the type of campaign that you need to work with.

Chapter 12: Creating a Video Campaign

Have you ever been on YouTube and seen an advertisement there? You may have seen something that was going to showcase a product or a service. A video ad is often seen as more memorable because it provides people with an interesting layout that offers more information.

The good news is that a video campaign can work in a lot of different places, not just on YouTube. And you can use these kinds of videos in order to help advertise within the Display Network as well.

There are a lot of reasons why you may want to work with a video campaign rather than some of the traditional methods of working with advertising. For example, your potential customers are more likely to recall information from a video campaign than the text they see in an advertisement. In addition, a video campaign can help you to get more information out there to your customer.

Many people will choose to use a video campaign in order to highlight demonstrations of the products or services that are for sale. It is also a great opportunity to answer any questions that your customers may have already started sending you.

Types of Video Ads

One thing that you are going to enjoy when it comes to working with video ads is that there are many different types of videos that you are able to use. Some of the video ads that you can consider using that can provide a different message and content based on what you want out of the advertisement include:

1. TrueView ads: These types of ads are the ones that are more prominent when you are doing a video campaign. These are going to show before, after, or during a video that is being displayed on YouTube, or in some other location on the Display Network. It is easy to get these ads noticed because they are posted right away online. The viewer is then able to skip the video after five seconds. What this means is that you want to make the video as attractive as possible to someone so they will keep on watching and then listen to your call of action.
2. Out-stream ad: These ads are the ones that show up on a tablet or mobile device. This would work also on a partner site of Google. The customer would just need to click on the video to get it to play.
3. Bumper ads: These ads are going to be shorter in length, usually six seconds or less, and you are able to find them in the same kinds of places as we found the TrueView ad. This provides you with a smaller window to contact someone, but it is also an ad that can ensure that your potential customer is able to see the content faster than before.
4. TrueView discovery videos: These videos are going to work only on YouTube, and someone needs to actively go in and click on your link. After the user clicks on the thumbnail for your ad, the video is going to play on a new screen. Think of this as a more voluntary approach, but it can help you get in touch with your customer simply by sharing details on what is being offered from your campaign at any given time.

How Do You Create the Video Campaign?

If you decide that the video campaign is the right option for you, then you must make sure that you produce good video ads, ones that are attractive and dynamic. These videos also need to look professional, or you will turn your customers off. If you don't have experience doing this on your own, then it is definitely something to consider hiring a professional to help you with.

Once the videos are done and they look like they are professional quality, it is time to do the following:

1. Go into your AdWords account and select on a new campaign option. From there, you are able to choose the video sections.
2. Specify the type of goal that you would like to attain. You do have a choice to not go with a goal right now and then you can change it later. When picking a goal, you can choose to get website traffic, get leads, or do more brand reach.
3. Select out the subtype for your goal. For instance, when you are working to get leads, you can choose to drive conversions.
4. Enter the name that you want to use for your campaign.
5. Set up the budget that you would like to spend each day or what you are willing to spend over the lifetime of your campaign.
6. Go through and decide the start and the end dates for the campaign that you are working on now.
    a. You have some options here. You can choose to let the campaign go as soon as possible. You can also choose to leave the end date blank when you just want to let it run for as long as possible.
7. Select the different networks that you would like to use. You can let the videos go on YouTube and on the Display Networks.
8. Choose the location and the language of the data. Don't forget about all of the advanced settings that are available, just like with the other options for campaigns that you choose.
9. Go in and select the bidding setup that works the best for your goals and your budget. Depending on the goal

that you have set up, you will have the option to work with conversion, impression, or cost per view. Include a total of how much you would like to send on these bids.
10. Use the content filter in order to determine the types of content that you aren't interested in having show up in the ads. This includes working with ratings for the content to appear on videos rated for certain audiences.
11. Set up the specific devices that you would like to have the videos display on. This could include mobile and desktop devices. You can always go through and change the settings section of the campaign at a later time. AdWords is going to put these options right out front when you begin the campaign in order to make things easier to work with.
12. Enter in the details of how many times you would like the ads to show up within a certain time frame. You can have this include the number of views and impressions as well.
13. Add in details on when you would want to have the ads in your pending ad groups appear. Details on the days of the week and specific hours for airing content should be included.

At this point, the video campaign should be created completely. You can then go to the dashboard and use the settings to change up the parameters that we just went through. This might include going through and changing the settings for the individual ad groups that you would like to produce for this campaign.

Loading the Videos That You Would Like to Use

Working with video campaigns will work a little bit differently than regular ads. Once you have the video ad done, and you have set up the group, you can prepare an actual aid for your content so that you can load up the videos and get them in front of the customers.

1. Start by making sure that you have connected YouTube to your AdWords account.
2. Go to the Ads and Extensions section of your video campaign page.
3. Click in order to create a new ad.
4. Select the ad group that you would like this ad to appear on.
5. Enter in the URL for your YouTube video. If you haven't uploaded the video to YouTube before this step, then now is the time to do it.
6. Select the video ad format. You can pick from out-stream, bumper, discovery, in-stream ad formats.
7. Now you can enter in the final URL. This is the place that you want people to go to when they click on the video.
8. Enter in the display URL for the video.
9. Along with the ad, make sure that you add in a call to action. This tells the customer what to do after the video is done. You are given ten characters for this.
10. Include a headline. This can be about 15 characters. This headline is going to appear on the small bar that lists information on who is providing the ad. Then the Call to Action will be distinct and provide the user with information on what makes the ad distinct.
11. Now you need to enter the name of the ad. You are given a maximum of 255 characters. This needs to be at the top of your ad.

After this, you should have the whole video campaign ad prepared. This will appear when it is linked to the keywords or other content that has been listed on the ad group that you assigned this video to. Be certain that the ad you created is a good one, something that your customer will remember and will share with others to get the best results from the work.

Remember that a good ad, especially a video ad, can be shared with a lot of different people if it is professional and really ads value to your customer. Make sure that you provide that value to your customer with each video that you create.

You should definitely spend some time working on video ads as part of your campaign. Even if you don't make a full campaign that deals with these videos, it is still a good idea for you to work with them. They can help you reach more customers. And if you make a high-quality video, you can make it viral and get a ton of different people to look at it, too. Make sure that if you go with these video ad campaigns, make sure that you check out the tips in this chapter to help you get started.

Chapter 13: Creating a Universal App Campaign

Everyone likes to work with mobile applications. They like how easy these are to load onto the mobile device and how you can purchase and use as many different kinds as you would like. In fact, there are many businesses who are creating their own apps so that it is easier for their customer to purchase the products or learn more about what they have to offer. It is no wonder why many groups that produce apps are so profitable in the business market.

Another method that you may want to try with your advertising campaign is a Universal App campaign. This one works well if your business has an app that you would like to promote. You can use this no matter what kind of app you are using, whether it is an Android or an iOS app. So, if you have a program that you would like your customers to download or that you would like them to use with an in-store purchase, then this is the right type of campaign for you.

The campaign that you use for these apps will appear on a lot of different sites. This can work well with YouTube, the stores that you provide your app for, and ads on the Google Display Network. This can also work if you want to advertise on regular searches with Google. Remember that the overall design of the campaign is to create a layout where you are able to get items promoted for downloading.

One thing to note here is that if you have the same app that works for both iOS and Android, you will still need to create separate campaigns for each one. You can work with the same parameters and the same audience for each campaign, but Google will require that you use separate campaigns to make it work.

Starting the Campaign

Before you are able to work with this kind of campaign, you have to make sure that you have the Google Play or the App Store already, depending on the platform that you want to work with. The steps that you need to take in order to get started with an app campaign includes:

1. Select the option for Universal App.
2. Select the platform that you want to use for the app, either Android or iOS. AdWords is not supported on Windows Phone or Blackberry.
3. Enter the name that you have for your app. Click on the specific icon and layout of the app that you would like to market.
4. Give your campaign a name.
5. You can then add up to four text ideas of 25 characters each. These lines of text need to be separated from each other. Google will use these lines in order to create ads with different layouts. This ensures you get ads that are unique and fresh. The best thing to do here is to check out the description you have posted on the app to see what you can use.
6. Check out the official name of the app and the icon. These are two features that you should have created after you get the app loaded onto the App Store or Google Play.
7. Choose to add in YouTube if you would like at this point. You can then enter in the URL that you use for the YouTube ad you want to use for this.
8. Load a maximum of 20 images for the ad. This is an optional feature that you can use, but it can really help to make the content more attractive and can bring in more customers.
9. Choose the languages and the locations that you would like to use with these ads.

10. You also need to select the standard that you would like to work with on your campaign optimization. This kind of optimization should focus on how the ad is able to reach people. You can use this to target all of the users, or any user you think would make an in-app purchase. In the beginning, you should focus on the in-app purchases or the install volume.
11. Add in details about the average budget that you are willing to spend on the campaign each day. Remember, you will pay up to your daily budget times 30.4, which is the average number of days that are in each month. You can also choose whether you want to spend the budget on the accelerated layout or the standard delivery method.
12. Enter the cost per install of the app. You want to keep this amount reasonable for how much you are willing to spend for every install of the app. Keep the targeted total below your actual value of the app, or where are you going to receive any profit when someone installs the app?
13. Add in the location types that you would like to target the most.
14. Select when you would like to run that campaign for. You can choose some specific dates to work with, or you can leave it open-ended and close it at another time.

You will find that this one is very easy to manage because there aren't as many options that come with it. If anything, the content you are going to use the most for this campaign should come from the link that you have either from the App Store or the Google Play listing that you created to hold your app and sell it. Your app will already have the details, the reviews, and the pictures with it if you filled in the listing page the right way. The ad that we are doing here is just introducing the readers to the content so they will decide to download it.

Again, remember that you have to create two separate campaigns if your app is available on each operating system. The iOS and Android platforms are going to work with different standards, which is why it is important to work with different campaigns.

Chapter 14: Linking Your Ad to Google Maps

Another thing that you may want to work with when creating an AdWords campaign is to link your business to Google Maps. Whenever you do a search through Google, you may notice that with some companies, there is a map that shows up on the screen. This can sometimes show up on the right-hand side of the browser or on the top of a mobile device. The map is going to display information on all of the businesses that are in that area that relate to that keyword.

This can be a beneficial way to market your business as people are able to highlight their specific product to others who are searching on Google pretty easily. You will find that the when you do this, you show up on the map and can get more customers than before.

People will use and benefit from the use of Google Maps on a daily basis. Your potential customers are going to search for information to find out if there is a certain business near them based on the keywords that they search. This can help provide details of what to find when looking for products or services in a local area. And you can use AdWords along with this feature to reach your customers better than ever before.

Start Out by Getting a Google My Business Listing

Before you are able to use all of the features that come with Google Maps, you must make sure that you have a Google My Business Listing. This listing is going to provide your potential customers with a lot of details on many things that relate back to your business including:

- Pictures of your business

- Pictures that can show the items and services that you offer.
- A link to the actual website that comes with your business.
- Any fax and phone numbers. These can include your mobile number and your traditional number if you want.
- Email contact information
- Daily hours of operation
- Links to social media sites that are associated with your company.
- A review site for any ratings that other customers have posted for your business.

There are also some extra things that can be shown on this page based on the type of business that you would like to link. For example, an auto dealer may want to list out some of the car types that they sell and some of the brands. A restaurant may be interested in including information on the food types that they serve.

Now that we know a bit more about some of the benefits that come with having this kind of listing it is time to go through some of the steps that are necessary to set up your own Google My Business listing:

1. Go to the website business.google.com to get access to this system.
2. Enter your listing into the network when you get to this system. Make sure that you add in as many details as you can here.
3. Enter the type of category that your business fits under. Google will have some categories that you are able to choose from. Enter a keyword for your business, and then take a look through the different categories to figure what one you want to work with.

4. List information on your delivery. You can first list whether you are able to deliver your goods and services. A place that doesn't deliver needs to have people visit the location.
5. Look through the information that you put in and then confirm it for Google for a review. It could take a few days before Google finishes the review on the content and then they will put it online.
6. Google is going to provide you with a verification code and you need to send this in either through email or regular mail. Google requires this in order to make sure that the person who is signing up for this business listing is the one who is actually responsible for the business. This is the way that Google ensures that the content and the information isn't stolen.

Getting Google Maps to Work

After you have had time to set up this new business listing, you get the chance to work with Google Maps. Your content is automatically going to show up on Google Maps but you want to work with AdWords in order to make that content more visible on the program.

If you want to make sure that your content is more visible on Google Maps, you need to start out with a brand new campaign. The steps that you need to take to make this happen includes:

1. Star by getting some location extensions applied to the account.
2. Start up a new campaign for the ad that you want to run.
3. You can then select either an Express or standard ad and then state that you would like to get people to reach a physical location. This option is going to open up a ton of parameters that you are able to use in order to get people over to your physical locates. His can also

ensure that the Google Maps system starts to work for you.
4. Next, we want to make sure that we are targeting the right location where we want to focus our marketing content. The location should be close to where the physical address of your business in. You can either go with a specific area for that or a radius that goes around the business.
5. Take some time to review any and all keywords that you would like to use. Remember that when you work with keywords, you need to pick out ones that are able to relate to the listing you have. They also need to be words that are competitive, and ones that your potential customer is genuinely going to use when they do a search.
6. From here, you need to set up your bid strategy. You can set up bids by location. As you set up the campaign, you need to prepare a listing for how much your bids will be, based on the physical location that the ad is going to appear on.
7. Confirm all of the data that you have placed into the campaign.
8. You will be asked to send in a verification note. This is a note that you will need to use for any map-specific ads. This will confirm that you are actually the one who runs the website for your ad. When you get the verification, you can then send the code back to Google, using the instructions that are included with the type of content that you are using.

This process does take some steps, and it does take a bit to confirm the information and deal with the verification process. But this process is also going to make it a whole lot easier to be visible through Google Maps. This is perfect when you consider how many other options and marketing tools are using Google Maps in order to promote your content. And it does wonders for making your content, and your website and company, more useful and attractive to the customer.

Chapter 15: Using the Keyword Planner

Entering the keywords and the right keyword match types that you would like to use on AdWords is going to ensure that you are able to get the most out of your campaigns. A good idea to help you pick out the right keywords and to get more out of the advertisements that you decide to use is through working with the Keyword Planner from Google.

The Keyword Planner is a tool that is available from Google in order to help you create a better campaign than before. It is a good way to research the keywords that you would like to work with, and it is free. Plus, it will work no matter what kind of ad set you decide to use it with.

In addition, you can use this tool to pick out as many keywords as you would like. Best of all, you don't have to add individual bid values to each keyword if you aren't interested in doing so. You just have to let the AdWords platform include all of those things into the same campaign, or even ad group, that you would like to target.

Understanding How This Marketing Tool Works

To start, the Keyword Planner is going to help you identify the types of keywords that you would like to add to your site. The planner will make it easier to find the keywords you need that are relevant to your goals when you create a campaign. The setup works for many marketers, such as those who are just starting out with a new campaign, and those who would like to have some extra help picking out the right keywords to use in the campaign.

In addition, you get the benefit of seeing some of the statistics of how some individual keywords have done. You can see what is making a keyword become more popular than before, and how many people have used that keyword each month over the last year. Using these traffic forecasts can give you a great idea of what is going on around you in the market, and can ensure that you are going to pick out the right keywords to reach your customers in no time.

How to Work with the Keyword Planner

The steps that you need to follow in order to start using the Keyword Planner includes:

1. Go to htps://adwords.google.com/aw/keywordplanner to get started with using this planner.
2. Enter in the phrases or the words, and even the URL, that goes with your business. You are able to work with as many of these as you would like. Google will provide you with some drop-down results for each item to ensure that the content you work with is accurate. Try to include as many good keywords as you can in this section so that you can diverse up your campaign ad.
3. Review the individual keywords that are listed on the page. You are going to see many keywords including items that are actually related to your chosen works, and some that are not as relevant.
4. Check out the competition that is involved with these keywords. When you pick out keywords that have a ton of competition, this means that you will need to spend more money and put more effort in to make your page visible. You should also look at the average number of monthly searches from each keyword. Some keywords may have over 10,000 searches or more each month.
5. Analyze the typical bid values that are tied to the keywords in your listing. The bid values would also involve the totals based on the low and high ranges of

each keyword. You may find that some are available for just $0.50 per click, and some may be as high as $5 a click. Google gets this information based on their projections for how many people will place a bid for that keyword.

6. Click on the checkbox for the keywords that you are the most interested in working with. You have the option to work with as many of these keywords as you would like. You could even click on each and every keyword on the screen, but this is not recommended. Some of the keywords that are there may not actually have any relevance to what you are looking for. Make sure to look at each and every keyword before you make a decision.
7. Click to add a particular keyword to a plan. You need to select the ad group that you want the chosen keyword to be added to. You can also select a keyword and let it be part of an exact, broad, or phrase match.
8. Now you need to click on the View Forecast button. This is going to show up on the bottom part of the screen after you have been able to add in one of your ad groups.
9. Review the details on what Google is forecasting for you. This forecast is going to be based on the keywords that you choose to use. The forecast is going to be a review of the potential clicks or impressions that you can get from a keyword. It is going to include the click-through rate that is going to give you a percentage of impressions that could become clicks.
   a. The top part of this page is going to include a full layout of every keyword that you are trying to use. The bottom will show you the individual results for every keyword. This can give you a good idea about how much you will spend when you use a particular keyword. You can always add in limits about how much you want to spend each day. This is just meant to give you

a general idea of what you might spend when you use that keyword.
10. Now we want to go through and download the keywords file in order to prepare a CSV file. This file is useful because it lets you save and then review the results of this particular search later. The file format can be put into Excel or another spreadsheet program that works for you. You can then take a look at it later on if you need.
11. Go to the overview section of the plan in order to get a full summary. The Plan Overview section is going to provide you with some extra information on not only what you may spend with the current plan, but also where you will find the content you post. You can also get information on the most likely devices ha the customer will use to search for the keywords. This helps you to configure your ads for either mobile or desktop use.

It is also possible for you to get some details on the location as well. This may be information on the most popular places in the country that some of your chosen keywords are going to be used. Naturally, when you take a look at this, the information is going to come from some of the bigger cities of the country, such as the Chicago, San Francisco, and New York markets. But it is just meant to be a rough estimate to help you out.

The overall process of working with the Keyword Planner is meant to help you look at some of the keywords that you are the most interested in, and then determine if they are actually smart choices or if something would work better for you. This tool can also give you some more details on the amount that you are likely to spend to get the results that you want out of your chosen keywords.

His is just meant to be a general guide for what you will need to do before you even start the AdWords campaign. Even when you already have a few keywords in mind that you would like to work with, it is still a good idea to put them into the Keyword Planner and see what results come up. You may find that a particular keyword has too much competition and is going to cost you too much in order to bid, or you may find more, or different keywords, that would be more effective for the work that you are trying to do.

Any time that you decide to work with the Keyword Planner tool along with your AdWords campaign, you will find that it provides you, whether you are an experienced marketer or someone brand new, a sensible plan that can make your marketing budget go further.

You will need to use this keyword tool any time that you would like to get the most out of the AdWords campaign that you are working with. This tool is going to give you a clear idea of how well the ads are laid out, how well they are going to function in the marketing plan that you have, and more—and since this tool is powered by Google, you know that you are getting the results that will matter the most for you.

Conclusion

Google AdWords is one of the top tools that you can use to market your products and services and even your company. There are a lot of other options to choose when it comes to promoting your business, but none of them offer as much reach as Google, as many options, and as much control over the budget and the way that the ad campaign goes for you.

This guidebook has spent some time exploring Google AdWords and how you can use it in your own business to see some amazing results. Everyone knows the Google search engine and all of the different parts that come with it. There is so much reach that comes with Google, and it is easy to reach your customers through this search engine, as long as you know where your customers are and can write convincing ad copy to bring them in.

There are a lot of different parts that come with using Google AdWords and getting the results that your business needs. This guidebook went through a lot of the different parts that come with a good AdWords campaign to help you get started on the right foot.

We looked at some of the basics first, with a good overview of what Google AdWords is all about and some of the benefits that come with it. We then took a look at some of the steps that you need to take to set up your own account.

Once all of those pieces are in place, it is time to move onto the different aspects that are needed to make a good AdWords ad. This includes tips on how to pick the right keywords, how to find and recognize the right target audience, and how to write out the best keywords to ensure you reach the audience that you want.

In addition, this guidebook is going to take some time to explore more about Google AdWords and creating the right campaign. We will also look at the right tips to set your budget in order to *really* get your ad ranked and bring in more people to your website.

After the budget is set, you have the right keywords, and you have written out effective ad copy—we need to explore some of the other aspects that come with being successful with your campaign. This guidebook spent some time exploring those as well, including how to work on an effective landing page to get more conversions, how to increase your Google Quality Score, and how to optimize your AdWords to get the most out of your campaign.

To help finish off this guidebook, we will also look at the ways that you can remarket your campaign to get more out of every ad, some of the best tips that you can follow to get more out of your AdWords, and some of the ways that expert marketers can get more out of their AdWords account.

There are a lot of different parts that come with running a good Google AdWords campaign, and as a beginner, it is sometimes confusing what is going to work the best for your needs. This guidebook has provided you with all of the tricks and information that you need to see success.

When you are ready to bring Google AdWords into your marketing campaign in order to see some great results with your sales and customer conversions, make sure to check out this guidebook to help you get started.

Now let's look at how to do SEO for beginners.

Part 2: SEO For Beginners

Introduction

How much you know about SEO at this point is irrelevant because in this book you will be guided from beginner all the way to expert on optimizing your search rankings in Google.

In the online marketing space there are two main sources of traffic that any given website can receive; paid and free. The great thing about paid traffic is that results can happen very quickly because you are buying the attention of your audience through means of social media, media buys, influencers and so on. If you have a great offer and can build trust fast a paid advertisement will outperform any free or organic traffic. However the biggest downfall and the reason most people focus in on using Google SEO for traffic is because unlike SEO, with paid traffic once you stop paying you stop the traffic. Almost like a faucet once your turn it off so does the water. SEO on the other hand acts as a waterfall, endless traffic 24/7 that can become highly sustainable over the long term for your business.

SEO takes time and for good reason, once it's all said and done organic traffic can change your entire business given enough search volume and search rankings. Ever since the beginning of Google SEO significant changes have been made to better the user experience of people who use Google to find information. Each year Google rolls out various changes to how their algorithms choose which websites rank to the top for any given keyword.

There are strategies that are long-term based for staying rank 1 for your keywords and may take effort in the beginning and there are also short term strategies that have a high risk of suffering penalties for your websites search rankings. In this book we will cover both short and long term strategies with an emphasis on long term also known as white-hat SEO.

There have been horror stories of websites making massive amount of money each month using short term strategies, also known as black-hat SEO, and eventually get caught by Google for taking shortcuts and losing all website revenue. The mindset going into SEO should be that of Google's mindset because if you do what Google wants, it will give you what you want (Rank 1 search). It will be important to learn how to do black-hat SEO so that you know what not to do and stay away from trouble at all costs.

The best use of this book is not necessarily creating notes of ideas you can use on your website right away but rather to implement what you learn immediately and come back to where you left off, that is how this book was designed.

So let's get into to it and talk about the most important factor of Google SEO: How the Google algorithm actually works in 2020.

Chapter 1: Understanding the Google Algorithm

This is arguably the most important section to learn about Google SEO. Once you understand what Google's algorithm looks for to push some websites as opposed to others to the top of search rankings then we can take appropriate actions to give our websites a high chance of getting to the top for our keywords.

Google actually gave this artificial intelligence a name when released in 2015, they named it RankBrain. RankBrain operates as a mass website sweeper that determines which websites rank above or below other for a given keyword. The algorithm looks at how users interact with searches and figures out which websites are being click based on relevancy, quality, and content. The 3 largest factors RankBrain looks for is number 1: Click through rate, exactly which websites are being clicked on for a specific keyword. Dwell-time: How long each user stays on a click website from a specific keyword, and lastly bounce-rate: how many viewers to a website leave after just the first page.

All this being said it goes without saying that Backlinks are the largest indicator of a websites authority. If you do not know what a backlink here is the definition: Backlinks are incoming clickable links to a webpage. When a website has on its website a link to another website basically saying "hey go to this website" or "check out this website", the website that is getting linked to actually gains authority in Google's eyes.

When trying to rank your website in Google for your keywords the majority of your SEO efforts must go towards gaining relevant, high quality backlinks so that Google will recognize your website as an authority for your keywords and rank you high. As mentioned not all backlinks are created equally. For example having a site about gambling link out to a website of a soccer blog would be a horrible backlink because Google will instantly notice the lack of relevancy between the two websites and end up punishing the linked website.

Likewise getting a backlink from a relevant website will do wonders for your SEO rankings in the eyes of Google because it indirectly suggests that you are the "go-to" website for that niche.

The most important quality of a backlink, is just that, the quality. Getting a backlink from a website that has a low 'domain authority' will provide you less credit that that of a high domain authority website would. For example getting a backlink from Forbes.com will surely give you better SEO compared to a backlink from a local blogger would.

One of the things that some websites do is offer high authority websites money in exchange for these amazing backlinks and this is what we call black-hat SEO which means it goes against all Google's terms of service and is subject to penalty. In this book we will discuss black-hat SEO strategies and white- SEO so that you learn the full spectrum of tactics.

It is worth noting that using any short cuts or black-hat SEO strategies will only grant you results temporally. In later chapters we will focus on white-hat SEO strategies that yield long term results for your business.

Another important factor that Google's algorithm looks for is your website's speed. Google feels a slow loading website deserves to rank lower because it is the first thing that provides a bad user experience for a website. Likewise fast loading websites are rewarded with higher rankings as they increase user experience. It is important to note that gaining a fast speed only ranks you higher at a certain point, or in this case a certain speed. Google has pointed out that nearly 25% of users will exit out of a website that takes 4 or more seconds to load and will also likely never re-visit that website again. Let's some about some strategies to increase your website's loading speed.

1. Your hosting company matter a lot. The host of your website has a huge impact on your websites load speed because some hosting companies priority fast servers while others do not. Most people are well of with popular hosts like GoDaddy or HostGator and will do good with them. However if you are in need to make a big upgrade to your websites page speed then the best hosting company in 2020 is WPEngine.com. The first issue people have is their high hosting prices and it is for good reason, when it comes to speed you get what you pay for and WP Engine's server are insanely fast.
2. Picture optimization: bigger files take much longer to download than smaller files. The majority of a website's weight lies in the images, so optimization of images can greatly affect your website speed. Along with proper sizing of images make sure to have each file type in JPEG format when uploading them onto word press. Quantity of images should be kept low because of this cardinal rule.
3. Your website Plugins. The number of plugin installed on your word press weighs a ton on the speed of your website. Unnecessary plugins add into the servers processing when loading a page and most website have plugins that are simply not needed. There is no exact number of plugins recommended because every website and business is different but as a general rule of thumb around 10 is considered normal.

On-page SEO

Optimizing your website for your SEO efforts is called on-page SEO and it takes up a chunk of your over rank factors when it comes to the Google algorithm.

Your URL's hold a heavy weight with on-page SEO, Google has confirmed the first few words in your URL hold the most weight for ranking factors and that longer spam looking URL perform less than short concise URLs.

Let's talk about the most important on-page SEO factor and the one you should spend the most time perfecting. Your website's Title Tag is the heaviest ranking factor and when done correctly can make changes to your SEO.

What you want to do is to put your keyword towards the beginning of your title tag and add words that add perceived value like "2020" or "best" or "guide".

As far as the content on your webpage goes the keys to pinpoint are your pages bounce rate and dwell time. Because these two ranking factors are so important to your on-page SEO there are a few content strategies that can help propel your information to higher levels.

Content tactic #1:

First and foremost images should be the first pieces of additional content added onto your website because they illicit more engagement with your readers and explain ideas in ways that sometimes text cannot do. High quality photos can be bought online if you do not participate in photography yourself. Stock image websites worth noting include Shutterstock.com, stock.adobe.com, and pexels.com.

Content tactic #2:

Embedding videos into your blogs and content can drive dwell time very high. Where most website owners get stuck on is they think they have to own a YouTube channel and embed their videos onto their website and while that may be a big advantage it is not the only way. Using other people videos can be a good way to add value to your content so long as you give credit to the owner of the said video and in some rare cases, permission.

For business owners with a high budget there are stock video websites available that provide a variety of video content. Pond5.com is where most content creators get their stock videos from because of the variety they offer with reasonable pricing.

Content tactic #3:

Diagrams and info graphics have proven to improve dwell times and SEO for content that is longer than just generic information. Very well written blogs have a lot of information that spell out ideas in a simple way along with diagrams just to make things that much easier for the reader. Infographics can be created by freelancers from as a low as 5 dollars up to 100 dollars. Fiverr.com is a great resource with getting these diagrams created and will ultimately help your content on your website look more professional.

Using your keyword in your content is crucial and but be done correctly otherwise you can get an SEO penalty from Google. Using your keyword too many times in your content should be avoided because Google sees this as manipulation so there should only be 1 mention of your keyword in the first 50 words of your content. Doing so will help Google understand what your web page is all about while at the same time not appear trying to trick the algorithm into over-relevance of that keyword.

Next up for On-page SEO is your Mobile friendly formatting. Google has put a higher emphasis on having a mobile friendly design over the last few years as the smart phone market has grown so much. Focusing on having a mobile design that responds well will have a positive effect on your rankings over the long term.

Designing a properly functioning mobile website can take a lot of know-how and in some cases may require hiring a professional. For the most part choosing a website builder that has existing mobile friendly templates is enough to not have it be an issue with your website responsiveness.

Linking out to other websites can be beneficial for your SEO because it lets Google know what your page topic is all about. Be sure to give at least 2 backlinks to relevant, high authority websites for every blog post you create as these sites being linked to reflect your webpage.

Along with send outbound back linking, incorporating inbound links in and around your website is a good thing for your on-page SEO. No more than 3 inbound links are necessary for a given blog post.

Social signals

Social media activity is on the low end for ranking factors in Google's algorithm but never the less should be looked at to gain a small advantage. The function of social signals are to spot the popularity of a piece of content via likes, shares, views and other forms of engagement on platforms like Facebook, Twitter, Pinterest, Instagram and so on.

If your business or website does not hold any social media accounts it is worth investing your time into creating and building them up. If you have existing social accounts be sure to imbed on-page elements to your website like Share button and Connect buttons. With these calls to actions your social media and website content can be cross promoted so your essentially pinging viewership over all platforms.

Social media platforms can grow from a variety of different strategies, here are some just to name a few:

1. Post consistently: It does not matter whether you are a business or just a website blog, you are showcasing a brand to the world. You always want to have your brand at the top of news feeds so the likelihood of engagement with your audience goes up. Different platforms have different consistency posting rates but keeping things simple to 1 post per day is enough to get the most out of your social accounts.
2. Images: Always use images when posting on social media. Too many content creators forget to post content with images on platforms like LinkedIn and Facebook and it only hurts your content's perceived value.
3. Hold contests: Giveaways and contests are the most commonly used strategies for growing a social account because it simply works. Hold a call to action after you announce your contest giveaway so that your audience knows they have to follow you or like a post in order to enter the contest.
4. Cross-promote: Use the leverage of other social accounts in your niche to form a partnership and promote each other's accounts to gain new followers very quickly.
5. Engage: Like, comment and respond to the feedback your audience gives you. This will generate a sense of

community for your social media that will have people coming back for future conversation.

With social media's rising popularity over the coming years it is bound to gain a higher ranking factor for your website's SEO.

Chapter2: Keyword and Competition analysis

Keywords are the words and phrases that your target audience actually type into Google. Knowing which words are being searched for can help you in your SEO because once you appear at the top of a Google search your website will flow with new people every day.

The first step towards your keyword research is to make a list of all the potential keywords you can think of. Try to create a list of 10-20 keywords and get inside the mind of your audience.

Doing your keyword research is critical to your SEO success. Keywords act as traffic sources that you choose to tap into and there a few things to keep in mind when choosing which keywords you decide to rank for. The most important metric for your keyword research will be its daily, monthly and yearly estimated volume. The worst things you can do in SEO is choose keywords that nobody searches for in Google and end up wasting a lot of your time. Any research tool you end up using will always just be an educated guess based on metrics that software has thought of to gain an accurate number of searches. There are a variety of different ways to see how often keywords are being searched for, let's go over 3 ways to find how much volume keywords get.

1. Moz.com offers a keyword explorer tool that has analytics on monthly search volume, click through rates, SERP (search engage results pages) analysis, and keyword suggestions. They currently offer 10 free searches per month and then the opportunity to upgrade to a paid version.
2. Google AdWords keyword planner tool has been introduced by Google themselves and can add a lot of value to the analytics of a keyword. The greatest asset

inside the Google keyword planner tool is you get to directly see how much each keyword is bidding for in Google Ads. This is relevant to us because it can showcase how much competition there is for a keyword and possibly even demand for some keywords.
3. Ahrefs.com is an expensive tool and is a very accurate software when it comes to monthly search volume even for smaller keywords. One really amazing feature inside Ahrefs is the ability to look at your competitors top web pages and see which keywords they are ranking for. This can give you an idea which keywords to look into. It can also let you know how your competitors are acquiring their backlinks but we will discuss getting backlinks in later chapters.

Short tail vs. long tail keywords

The difference between a short tail and long tail keyword is a short one contains 1-3 words while a long one has 3+ words. Shorter tail keywords are more difficult to rank for because they are generally more broad and tend to get much more traffic. Longer tail keywords are easier to rank and get much lower search volume, although they tend to convert much higher.

There is a middle ground of middle tail keywords whereby the search phrase is relatively short but very specific, an example for this would be "dog toys California". There are only 3 words but its more likely to convert into a reader/customer merely for its specificity. For your SEO efforts its recommended to have a mix of short to long tail keywords so that you can capture more traffic to your one website.

One of the best ways to discover the best keywords for your website is to understand all the problems that you content or products solve. List out all the phrases, adjectives and other words that describe the benefit or solution to their problem.

One metric that is paramount to understand because choosing your keywords that you want to rank is the difficulty of ranking a keyword. If a big brand has all the top spots then it would not be worth your time and money to try and rank for such difficult keywords. If you have selected your keywords and are ready to begin creating content and acquiring backlinks first look at the backlinks of all the top results in the search engine for your keywords and decide whether you are prepared to compete with them or not. For example if most of top results for a keyword have low domain authority and each webpage has 30 referring backlinks then yes it would make sense to compete. However if you run into high domain authority websites with referring domains of 300 for example it would be too challenging to pursue. If you are entering a competitive market start with smaller, easier to rank keywords to get your foot in the door and build authority on your website before jumping into more difficult keywords.

Re-evaluating your keywords every 3-4 months will keep you on top of your numbers and can help you take actions against any changes in your market relating to keywords. If it has been at least 6 months since your keyword research you may find crucial changes like using new keywords or dropping irrelevant keywords.

Chapter 4: White hat and black hat strategies

Acquiring backlinks will be the best indicator of your SEO over a long period of time. Before you begin gaining new backlinks it is important to know short term policies that Google has said they do not like. The biggest reason to understand black hat strategies is so you can avoid them and not suffer any penalties from Google over the course of your back linking efforts. There are however some businesses that operates on trends and are in and out with websites so short term SEO strategies make more sense. The following strategy is extremely effective and should only be done with caution. Let's talk about what a PBN is or a private blog network.

PBN's

A private blog network is a series of websites owned by one person with the sole purpose of creating backlinks to a primary 'money' website. Your money website is the target website that you want to rank in the end and every other website you have is in a blog format with content and your intention is to imbed backlinks that link back to your money site.

The trick here is not to create multiple websites on your own, build up their authority, and then use them as backlinks. That would just take too long and would not be worth it. What we do here is purchase domain names that are expired, but still hold authority. From this we can bypass all the time and effort it would take to build a website's authority and just purchase it instead. There are two primary ways to acquire expired or expiring domains, the first being purchasing them on auction websites and the second going through a broker. Using auction websites is more for finding domain names that are going to expire soon, the ones already expired are usually picked up by competitors very quick. There are many different auction sites to choose from, here are 3 popular ones that hold high volume expiring domains. 2 starting places are directly on the domain registrars GoDaddy and NameCheap. You can find both URLs by typing GoDaddy auctions or NameCheap auctions into Google. The third option is to use namejet.com. These 3 options are enough to get you started in your expiring domain research and begin building your private blog network.

We can check the domain authority of a website by using Ahrefs.com or smallseotools.com/domain-authority-checker. Most PBNs look absolutely terrible because some people just don't care how they look and don't care to get caught by Google. If you want to create a high quality PBN that will last you a long time then you will need to use this exploit with care. Buy your expired domains names, and use different hostings for each new website purchased. Connecting your internet to a VPN (or virtual private network) will ensure the highest safety possible with regards to your location being exposed. Build up the websites, write really good content on them and give the website a good design to it. By doing this in the eyes of Google's you are a real blog giving real value to your market but of course they do not know that you own all these beautiful websites and are linking back to the real website that you want to rank up in the Google search engine. To avoid the risk of getting penalized link out on each private blog only once or twice. Over use to backlinks that link back to your money website will most definitely get your money website de-indexed from Google. There should also be some pages with no links at all and some with links being sent out to other relevant high quality websites. Do not begin linking out to your money website from the first post, instead create the other posts with backlinks to really good websites first. It also goes without saying that every single anchor text be different. An anchor text for a backlink is the hyperlinked words used to send a backlink to a website. There are different variations you can use when linking out to a website so let's go over 6 of them; the first type of anchor text is naked URL backlink. With this type of text the full URL website address is being hyperlinked on a post so a person who clicks that link will know before time the exact full URL they will be re-directed to. An example would be the following: http://www.example.com/example-anchor-text. The second type of anchor text is the exact-match backlink. This type of backlink is a hyperlinked text that uses the exact keywords the website is trying to rank for. An example would be an anchor text of "Red Dog Toys" linking to a page about red dog toys. The third type of anchor text is the generic type whereby the anchor texts used are most commonly "Click Here" or "This Website" or any other generic phrase implying to click on the link. The 4th type is an image anchor text. Google will use the ALT tag as the anchor text for an image that you imbed on a page. The 5th type is a partial-exact match anchor text. Just as the name suggests the phrase used partially matches the keyword that is being ranked for. An example for linking to a dog toy website would be something like "Read this dog toy article". The last anchor text is branded. Brand names can be used as anchor text to link out to a website and is more commonly used in a more generic manner. An example would be Check out "Pampers" to see their full selection of baby diapers.

The bulk of you backlinks should be naked and branded backlinks because naked links are deemed as very safe by Google since there is immediate transparency and branded links because Google wants you to focus on brand building because they last longer than most links.

Structuring your website

Depending on your niche you will have specific pages you need to create, but here are the standard pages that are a must when creating your private blog website:

1. Contact Us – When creating this page explain the best way for your audience to reach you and include a basic contact form that can be installed inside word press.

Adding an email address is the best way to show your availability.
2. About Us – With this page write about the reason for the creation of the website and the problem it intends to solve for your niche. Include short biographies of yourself and/or your team.
3. FAQ – This section will depend on your niche and should include the most commonly asked questions your audience has about the content on your blog.
4. Privacy policy/terms and condition – This page is self-explanatory, privacy policies are legal statements that show how much permission is given to the public for use of content on a website. All legitimate websites have one which why your website will benefit from one.

With this information of creating private blog networks you should begin acquiring and owning a variety of blogs with authority that you can safely link back to your primary money website to boost its search rankings. Aside from creating your own network of private blogs there are 2 other options for marketers with a high budget that want to speed things up. The first is to actually pay an expert to build an entire network for you. You can find expert on freelance websites like Upwork or use SEO specific websites. The 2nd alternative to building your own network is to find existing private blog network and use their websites to buy links from. I would only suggest this option if you are sure the seller is reputable and their network of blogs is relevant to your niche.

Chapter 5: Link Building Strategy

In this chapter we will discuss strategies to gain the most backlinks with high domain authorities to ensure Google figures your website as an authority website. Backlinks are the backbone of your over search engine ranking. Before we can cover which backlinks to squire and how to go about getting them we must first go over which links to avoid that could potentially damage our domains ranking. The first type of backlinks to watch out for is irrelevant links pointing to your website in a different niche. Google expect links to be built naturally over a long period of time. Irrelevant backlinks directed to your website will show Google that you have just received an inorganic link pointed towards your website and clearly will and no direct benefit to the end user.

There are only two kinds of backlinks in the SEO world: Do-Follow backlinks and No-Follow backlinks. The only difference between the two is that one link will send authority to a website, and the other will send zero authority to a website. You see, in the eyes of Google if someone creates a blog post and inserts an anchor text with a link directed towards a website, that blog post owner has the option of sending that website any link juice, or "authority". In the backend of a website in the HTML section a backlink that does not direct link juice will be identified as "nofollow". All web 2.0 websites are automatically set to no-follow because the website has openly made linking public so anyone can just link their own website. For example if you create a Facebook business page and link and insert your website link on that page you will be given zero link juice because Facebook is an example of a web 2.0 website. The same goes for all social media websites and any website that has the intention of user created content, like blog websites. Your SEO strategy must include acquiring both nofollow and dofollow backlinks. Reason being both type of backlinks would happen organically for any website so Google will legitimize any website that has both. Websites with only Do-Follow backlinks are clearly attempting to manipulate the algorithm and will be punished over the long term in their respective search rankings. The ratio that most big company website use is 80:20 and that is the ratio that will ensure the most safety in 2020 for your overall backlink profile. There are 3 types of websites are will have the most direct benefit in term of quality backlinks being sent to your website. 2 of them are do-follow and 1 is no follow, the first 2 are company websites and blogs. These two types of websites often hold the most authority and will be the primary focus of your link building strategy. Big companies inherently hold high value to Google so they will be the most difficult but most rewarding types of do-follow backlinks to acquire. Most blogs on the internet are small but because of the vast quantity a lot have made it big with a lot of authority. Most of the backlink strategies will involve blog backlinks. The 1 other type of website is no-follow and this type of backlink will be social backlinks. These includes your own links from your websites social profiles, and any shares that your posts get from other people such as Facebook post shares, Instagram shout outs, Twitter shares and so on.

Purchasing excess "private blog network" backlinks can compromise the visibility of the network you purchase from which will ultimately result in you losing any links pointed towards your website. The objective of a PBN is to remain private so as soon as a large network of hidden websites starts selling links to the public it essentially becomes a public blog network. A few red flags a PBN will not be worth investing in are the following:

1. The content on each page is incredibly low. Pages with fewer than 800 words tend to underperform with SEO since Google's algorithm favors heavy content.
2. There are far too many links being sent out on each page. Low quality private blog networks have too many backlinks being sent out on each page and it signals to

Google the only purpose of this post was to send link juice to all these other websites.
3. The last mistakes PBNs will make are the links being irrelevant to the website's topic.

If you are ranking for keywords in very high demand and a lot of competition some PBN links may the worst kind of links you can acquire. Smaller keywords, especially local keywords benefit the most from PBN because they have a fast response time on keywords that are not searched for a lot but still have high profit potential for your website. For example ranking for a plastic surgery website in a town with a population of 40,000 people would benefit greatly from private blog backlinks because of the limited exposure that business will have for plastic surgery keywords. In later chapters we will cover local SEO strategies more in-depth.

Blog comment sections also hold risk with backlinks because of their dirty history. Backlinks from posting on other people blog posts in the comment section used to be abused by SEO strategists and were spammed all over the web. Google took strict actions and made comment links hold far less weight in link juice and are most of the time No-follow links.

Let's first discuss acquiring nofollow backlinks from social profiles since they are the easiest to gain.

The worst thing a business can do for their website is create social media profile, insert their websites URL, and just leave it be. Any link inserted on a social platform or any web 2.0 website should contain 2 factors: Content and frequency.

When building out your social profiles Google recognizes which business pages have more authority over other based on how frequent you create content, how many likes, shares, and comment you receive from your content and the overall engagement from that social platform.

We are very lucky for all the various software that exists on the internet that takes care of automatic social posting on many different platforms. Larger businesses can just outsource their entire social media marketing to a team or an agency but for smaller websites and businesses they will have to do it on their own. Some softwares that offer automatic posting of content are Hootsuite.com, HeyOrca.com, and AgoraPulse.com just to name a few. Social media authority is not the biggest component of your SEO rankings but should not be overlooked and be handled correctly for serious rankers. Your two objectives here with nofollow backlinks are to appear as an authority and to appear natural to Google, and that's exactly what social links will do for you.

Now let's talk about strategies for acquiring high quality dofollow backlinks

1. *Guest Blogging*. These types of backlinks are the most common because there are a plethora of blogs on almost every single niche on the internet. The premise behind this strategy is to find relevant blogs and get in contact with the website owner by either going into the contact us section of the blog or going to whois.com and searching for any form of contact available and asking the blogger to publish a post on a topic you are knowledge on and have him link to your website or just give the person a fully done blog post with your embedded anchor text all ready to go. Before going in for the pitch it is always much easier to first do something for your target blogger and give value. However if the person agrees to take your blog and publish it on his website then you are already giving value with free content.
A good starting place for guest blogging is using big networks like MyBlogGuest.com or BloggerLinkUp.com.

These blog networks connect blog owners who are seeking experts on a topic to create content in exchange for dofollow backlinks.

2. *Internal linking*. This tactic is often overlooked but it holds importance for your overall backlink profile. Not only do you have complete control on which links are linking each other on your own website but it actually help Google crawl your website much faster and index your pages.
3. Free and Paid Directories. Some directories allow dofollow links and other have it set to nofollow. More often than not the paid directories have more dofollow opportunities. Be sure to only submit your website's details to directories that are in your niche. Alltop.com is a blogger directory that will accept your website. To find highly relevant directories search in Google "your niche" + directory and you should have a list of free and paid directories to choose from.
4. Relationship Links.

    One of the most lost term link building strategies one can acquire is a relationship with a website writer or owner who has a high domain authority. Facebook groups are the easiest way to find people with similar interests and websites filled with content that are relevant to yours. Think first of how you can add value to a website owner before asking for any kind of backlinks. Some beginner things you can give a website owner would be photos that you own and that are high quality. If for example you want a relationship with a real estate website owner and you have great pictures of homes that he/she can add to their website then start with that.

5. Testimonial Links.

    Many companies love getting new testimonials because if increases the credibility of their business which often leads to more sales. In your emailing efforts with website owners offer a legitimate testimonial whether that be in written form or in video form they will truly appreciate it and the opportunity for a link will be open.

6. Analyzing your competitors' backlinks.

    There are a lot of SEO software and tools available to you that can give you information on competitor websites. The information included in these softwares are the source of their backlinks, which leaves an opportunity for you. If you notice a common link they are acquiring then why can't you also get it? Assuming they are in the same niche as you, you can go after backlinks that your competitors have. Ahrefs.com and SEMrush.com and two great tools to start with.

7. Resource page links.

    Recourse pages on websites are pages that link out to content on a given category. Since their sole purpose is to link out they make excellent backlinks. Once you find a resource link on that website that matches content you have on your website you can go ahead and send an email with a request to link to published content on your website.

That ends the beginners guide to SEO. You should have enough information to begin ranking your websites to the number one result in Google. SEO is a long term strategy for internet traffic so patience and strategy are key. For more information please visit my friends over at Moz.com for additional information on your SEO efforts.

CPSIA information can be obtained
at www.ICGtesting.com
Printed in the USA
LVHW081605281119
638857LV00016B/434/P